GLYNDŴR
- *The Ess*

Celia
and Ian Skidmore

GWASG CARREG GWALCH

ISBN: 0 86381 093 4

*First published in 1988 by Gwasg Carreg Gwalch,
Capel Garmon, Llanrwst, Gwynedd,
Wales.
Tel: 06902 261*

Celia and Ian Skidmore are broadcasters, TV presenters, authors and journalists. Together they run the aptly named "Two's Company" PR Consultancy. Celia won the 1988 Tir Na N'og Wales' premier prize for children's literature for her book.

They were retained by Glyndŵr District Council to create a corporate image for its £150,000 three year scheme to attract holiday-makers. Writing for travel magazines about places they knew — they met at Llangollen Eisteddfod — discovering places they had never been to, didn't seem to do justice to this lovely part of Wales. They set out to write the book, not as a PR exercise, but as a labour of love.

WHO WAS OWAIN GLYNDŴR?

The last native Prince of Wales was not a usurper. Owain Glyndŵr was a direct descendant of a famous Welsh hero, Bleddyn ap Cynfyn, Prince of Powys and of Gwynedd, who reigned at the time of the Norman Conquest of England. In 1159 the Princedom of Powys was split in half and Owain's ancestor Madog ap Gruffydd was given Powys Fadog, the country of the Dee and the Ceiriog. He shrewdly surrendered his lands to King Edward I when it became obvious that Wales' days of independence were numbered and swiftly regained them as a tenant in capite to the king. When he died he left his lands equally divided between two sons. In the custom of the day the king made the sons wards of two of his nobles, the Marcher barons Warren and Mortimer. Both boys disappeared and their lands were inherited by their guardians.

Perhaps it was conscience which caused Warren in 1282 to petition King Edward to grant the manors of Glyndyfrdwy, near Corwen, and Cynllaeth in the Tanat Valley to the boys' surviving relative, an uncle.

Five generations later Owain inherited.

On his mother's side Owain was descended from another princely line, that of Deheubarth. Her sister married Tudur ap Goronwy, and founded the Tudor dynasty from which the British royal family is descended.

Outside Wales little is known of Glyndŵr beyond the one-dimensional figure of the Shakespeare play. Those who have heard of him often see him in romantic terms as a robber chieftain; the Victorian balladeers were even less complimentary. To them he was a club-wielding barbarian in a sheepskin.

In fact he was a poet, a lawyer, a general in the English army, a charismatic warrior in the John Wayne mould. He was the richest Welshman in the land. But above all he was a polished and courteous gentleman. A parfit gentil knight.

In the ballads which were the pop music of his day he was Sir Owen, the Knight of the Glen. He was an authority on the chivalric code. On September 3, 1386, he gave evidence at a Court of Chivalry convened in Chester to settle a dispute over ownership of a coat of arms between two powerful families, the Grosvenors and the Scropes. The trial was the longest and the most famous in medieval England. It lasted four years and every famous knight in the land gave evidence. Among them, at the age of 27, 'Oweyn, Sire de Glendore'.

On the death of his father Owain's family came under protection of Richard Fitzalan, the Earl of Arundel, whose March of Chirkland was next to Owain's smaller March. Records show that he was a good guardian. Immediately after her husband's death Arundel lent the widow money, took Owain into his household at Chirk Castle, nominally as a page but in fact to train as a soldier.

It may have been Arundel who financed the boy as a student at the Inns of Court in London, the accepted education for a gentleman, as indeed were the years of service as a page. It was the custom of the day for seven-year-old boys of the warrior caste to be enrolled as servants in noble households. The code of chivalry held that those who were to govern wisely must first learn to serve. So the pages did their masters' bidding and in return were encouraged to play war games and learn their soldiers' trade.

His training at Chirk turned Owain into a formidable soldier and gave him his first taste of rebellion. As page to the Earl he fought at the battle of Radcote Bridge against

Richard II's favourite, the Earl of Oxford. But for most of his lifetime Owain was loyal to the English crown. In 1383 he fought the Scots in the English army led by John of Gaunt. Glyndŵr was the hero of the day. One ballad describes how when his lance was splintered he fought on using the splintered butt as a dagger and driving the Scots before him 'like a flock of goats'.

It was not until he was middle-aged, living peacefully at his manors by the river Tanat and the Dee, that Owain led an army against his king, though a different king to the one to whom he had given a lifetime's service. Richard II had been deposed by Henry IV when Owain went to war in 1400.

The war began with a squalid land-grab by Owain's other neighbour, Lord Grey of Ruthin. Grey laid claim to a stretch of barren moorland above Corwen. Glyndŵr protested to parliament but his petition was rejected. 'What do we care for these barefoot Welsh dogs?' one noble taunted.

He was soon to care very much indeed.

Back in Wales Owain made his plans. Bards went about the country recruiting an army. On September 16, 1400, he was crowned Prince of Wales at his manor house on the banks of the river Dee. His first raid on Ruthin was bloodless but the town suffered heavy damage; his Tudor cousins captured Conwy Castle.

In the years that followed Glyndŵr took his war to mid-Wales and then to the South. He fought and defeated his patron, the Earl of Arundel; captured some castles and laid siege to others. He made alliances with the French, but for whose disastrous intervention he might have conquered all Britain. As it was he got as far as Gloucester, which he looted. In 1405 he was the undisputed master of Wales. By 1409 it was all over. A year earlier the English had recaptured Harlech Castle from which he had ruled. Though Owain and one son escaped, his wife and two daughters were captured and sent to the Tower of London where they died of starvation.

11

In 1415 Owain disappeared from history. In fact he went to live in quiet retirement at Kentchurch Court in Herefordshire with his daughter Catherine who had married one of his former enemies, Sir John Skydmore.

Sir John, if history is to be believed, was a plausible rogue. After his wedding he sued the Crown for the return to his wife of her family estates, sequestered during the rebellion. But the Crown was not having any. The Glyndŵr fortune was already dispersed, divided amongst the King's Beaufort relatives. It is nice to have an ancestor who is a trier. And it doesn't really matter who owned it half a millenium ago... Nowadays we can all enjoy Glyndŵr Country.

Llanrhaeadr Waterfall   Photo: Peter Griffiths, Oswestry

THE TANAT VALLEY

There are many ways into the hidden land of the Tanat Valley. Beguilingly, via its neighbouring valley the Ceiriog, smoothly from Oswestry. Or boldly from Bala, round the hem of the Aberhirnant Forest, through the Milltir Cerrig Pass at a height of 1,638 feet. The road drops from the pass at the head of the Eiarth Valley to the village of Llangynog, across a wooden bridge at the foot of Craig Rhiwarth. Even on the balmiest days in spring and autumn there is a frisson of danger in the descent. In winter it can be downright hazardous.

Most heart-in-the-mouth journeys are better enjoyed in retrospect after the anguish is over. Fortunately in Llangynog there is a splendid haven for retrospection. It is called the New Inn and like all 'New Inns' it is one of the oldest buildings in the village. The drovers used it. In the eighteenth century the drivers of the pack teams which brought the outside world to the Tanat paused there: to wonder, no doubt, if the outside world was worth repeating the journey for. Their problem and the peculiar charm of the Tanat is that having reached it you only have very vague memories of what the outside world is like.

Bala one may recall, the Aberhinant Forest and the exciting miles of the uplands drive. The view of the Aran mountains across the apparently endless moorland above the tree-line is unforgettable. The first moment on the crest of Milltir Cerrig goes beyond memory. It is imprinted on the soul. To the east Moel Sych, at 2,713 feet the highest of the Berwyn peaks, and to the west the wide, flat valley floor down which the Eiarth runs, thin as white darning wool. But beyond that the world of cities and bustle is as remote as Tibet. So quiet is the Tanat; so empty its roads of traffic, that when at last it is left the pleasant market town of Oswestry will seem a metropolis, choked by cars.

Pleasantly rural Llangynog was once a thriving industrial community. In 1692 a rich vein of lead was found which was three and a half yards wide. Unfortunately, after it had been dug a hundred yards, water made further mining impossible. But for forty years the lead mine earned its owner, the Earl of Powys, the fabulous income, in the seventeenth century, of £40,000 a year. In the eighteenth century a slate quarry was discovered but never fully exploited. There were no means of carrying the slate away by water nor transport powerful enough to carry it over the pass.

Nowadays Llangynog's chief claim to fame is that it is the gateway to Cwm Pennant, a beautiful valley which is also the cradle of a charming mixture of myth and history. To unravel its secrets collect the key to the church of St Melangell which is kept in a cottage behind the village newspaper shop in Llangynog. But before visiting the church drive to the farm gates at the head of the valley. From there you can see the first of the Berwyn's many cataracts, the Falls of Tanat.

The river rises some miles further up in the loneliest and highest Berwyn moorlands — 2,000 feet above sea level — between Lake Vyrnwy and Lake Bala. It reaches its valley by tumbling hundreds of feet down Craig Wen, the *White Crag*. It touches the valley floor on private farmland. Hardy travellers who wish to inspect it at closer quarters must first ask permission at the farm and be prepared to wade across a stream and through a considerable bog.

Less hazardous and highly rewarding is a visit to the church of Pennant Melangell and the shrine of St Melangell, the patron saint of hares. There are many versions of her story but space here for only two. The first was written by Thomas Pennant who toured Wales on

16

horseback in the eighteenth century and wrote a fine guide
to the country...

> At about two miles distant from Llangynog I
> turned up a small valley to pay my devotions to
> the shrines of St Monacella or, as the Welsh style
> her, Melangell.
>
> Her legend relates that she was the daughter of
> an Irish monarch who had determined to marry
> her to a nobleman of his court. The princess had
> vowed celibacy. She fled from her father's
> dominions and took refuge in this place where
> she lived fifteen years without seeing the face of
> man. Brochard Yscythog, prince of Powys,
> being one day a-hare hunting pursued his game
> till he came to a great thicket; when he was
> amazed to find a virgin of surprising beauty,
> engaged in deep devotion, with the hare he had
> been pursuing under her robe, boldly facing the
> dogs who retired to a distance, howling,
> notwithstanding all the efforts of the sportsmen
> to make them seize their prey. Even when the
> huntsman blew his horn, it stuck to his lips.
> Brochwel heard her story and gave to God and
> her a parcel of lands to be a sanctuary to all that
> fled there. He desired her to found an abbey on
> the spot. She did so and died abbess in a good
> old age.

The poet Robert Southey told the story charmingly in a
rhyming letter to his daughter:

> Tis a church in a vale, whereby hangs a tale, how
> a hare being pressed by the dogs and much
> distressed, the hunters coming nigh and the dogs
> in full cry, looked about for someone to defend
> her, and saw just in time, as it now comes pat in

17

rhyme, a saint of the feminine gender. The saint was buried there, and a figure carved with care, in the churchyard is shown, as being her own; but 'tis used as a whetstone (like a stone at our back door), till the pity is the more (I should say the more's the pity if it suited with my ditty) it is whetted half away — lack-a-day, lack-a-day. They show a mammoth rib (was there ever such a fib) as belonging to Saint Melangell. Was there ever such a wrangle, and tell the simple people that if this had been her bone, she must certainly have grown, to be three times as tall as the steeple.

Nowadays both stone and bone lie in the church next to the gravestone effigy of a knight in armour, Madog ab Iorwerth. A frightened hare peeps from beneath the saint's waist belt. Not surprising. Iorwerth, whose sword is half drawn, was the son of Rhirid the Wolf.

Not that there was any great danger. In the valley hares are traditionally known as 'St Melangell's lambs' and it is said that if anyone who sees a hunted hare cries 'St Melangell be with thee', escape is assured. Behind the statues is a 15th century rood screen with a charming carving telling the fable. A flashlight is essential.

Beyond the church is the rock slab known as St Melangell's bed, where her Latin name 'Monacella' is carved in the stone. More accessible is her shrine in what was for many years the vestry, though always known as the Cell of the Grave. In 1958 excavations disclosed under the wooden floor a much earlier stone and rubble floor. Below that floor again the archaeologist came upon cobbles and a grave slab which covered human bones. These now rest in the raised shrine which includes fragments of the masonry of the original stone reliquary, thought to date back to the twelfth century.

Connoisseurs of falling water will find another cascade of equal grandeur to the Tanat in the next valley to the south. The river Goch becomes Pistyll Gyfyng as it tumbles down the rocks of Tap-y-Gigfran (the Tap of the Raven). However it can only be reached on foot and with difficulty from a path just below the bridge at Llangynog. This is Ellen's path, probably a road made by Stone Age man and adapted by the Romans who mined these hills. Ellen of the Roads, the legendary wife of Macsin, a Mabinogion visionary prince, is almost certainly an allegory of the Roman road builders.

In the Middle Ages protection to the pilgrims along the valley floor was given by the Knights Hospitaller. Anyone bold enough even today to walk the narrow mountain path to the Tap with a precipitous drop into the valley might feel that even those bold knights would not be protection enough against the danger.

Most travellers will prefer the more famous, and infinitely more accessible, grandeur of Pistyll Rhaeadr.

This, one of the Seven Wonders of Wales, is reached from the large village of Llanrhaeadr-ym-Mochnant, famous chiefly because it was in a summer house here, above the parish church of St Dogfan, in the reign of Elizabeth I, that Bishop William Morgan, whilst still a parish priest, translated the Bible from Hebrew and Greek into Welsh. The first Welsh Bible was published in 1588 and in gratitude the Queen made Morgan Bishop of Llandaff.

Morgan spent ten years translating the Bible in the pavilion among the trees at Pen-y-Walk at Rhaeadr. His parishioners, who knew nothing of the work, assumed that he spent his time there sulking and refusing to perform his pastoral duties.

The sad truth is that his parishioners were glad to see him go. The Rev. Morgan was so unpopular that at service time he was escorted from his home — now Llys Morgan, a delightful and hospitable guest house, run by a descendant of the Bishop — to the church, less than a hundred yards away, by an armed servant. He preached his sermons with a pistol stuck in his belt.

Morgan was born in 1549 in the Wybrnant Valley at Penmachno. Even today, refurbished by the National Trust to celebrate the four hundredth anniversary of the publication of his Bible, it is difficult to reach. When Morgan's family lived there as poor tenant farmers (their official description was 'slave-tenants') it must have been virtually inaccessible. Which leads to speculation as to why young Wil Morgan was taken up by the squire, Morris Wynn of Gwydir Castle. He was taught first by the squire's own chaplain and later installed as an undergraduate at St John's College, Cambridge.

Morgan's troubles began when he married a prosperous widow, Catherine Lloyd, thus incurring the wrath of her brother Ifan Meredith, who, by the marriage, lost her estate. Things got worse when the luckless vicar arranged another marriage between his patron Morris Wynn's son John and another Catherine, this time the daughter of a local landowner, David Lloyd ap William. For Ifan Meredith had wanted her for *his* nephew, an attorney called Edward Morrice.

Work on the Bible went on against a background of lawsuits, feuding families and bitter recrimination. The year after the translation was completed the trouble came to a head when Ifan Meredith led an attack against the Rev. Morgan and the village militia he was training, laying siege to the vicarage.

In actions before the Star Chamber which followed the details of the feud were aired. The vicar accused Meredith of living with a lewd woman, Margaret Ellis. She was, he claimed, 'a woman known to be very lewd (being arrayed in her worst apparel as one ready to scramble and skirmish and having in her company certain stout women with their aprons full of stones) for what she could not accomplish with her hands she left not unaccomplished with her tongue.'

As well as the attack on the militia the Rev. Morgan accused Meredith of assaulting his curate, Lewis Hughes. Meredith denied the charge claiming that he had only visited the curate to borrow a harp. For good measure he accused the curate of being reckoned lewd and 'a great alehouse knight'.

The vicar won the first round but the legal battle went on until Sir John Wynn finally settled it at some cost to the vicar.

Llanrhaeadr is more peaceful now, if a village which boasts 23 separate committees and is administered by four different councils can be said to be peaceful. But the alehouse knight will not need to look far for a tavern or a tournament. George Borrow, who marched through Wales in the nineteenth century bowed under the weight of his own ego, chose the Wynnstay Arms opposite the church. He liked what he found and spoke kindly of the landlord. It is still welcoming and the landlord, a very knowledgable countryman, will talk happily for hours about the Berwyns and their wildlife.

Perhaps it was here that the curate Lewis Hughes won his spurs in the alehouse lists or perhaps at the Hand Hotel, a welcoming inn of warm stones, ancient beams and huge fireplaces.

The Hand is a family affair, a family so devoted to the Tanat that when they emigrated to Canada 21 years ago they flew back every year for a caravan holiday in the Valley. Every year, that is, until three years ago when among their holiday shopping they found, rather to their surprise, they had bought a pub. Now, with some relief, they are home for good.

Unlike mine host of the Wynnstay, the Baines family at the Hand are not professional innkeepers. Tony Baines was a toolmaker, his son Martin was a lithographer and Mrs Doreen Baines was an accountant. Her Latvian daughter-in-law, Ruta, is the only one with experience of a hotel. But what they lacked in know-how they have been making up for with enthusiasm.

In three years they have restored a nondescript pub to its original sixteenth century ambience, including a fireplace so huge there are cushioned benches inside it. Perhaps in its early days, disgruntled parishioners sat there plotting the downfall of the Rev. Morgan.

The Tanat beckons people from the far corners of the earth. When Lorraine Pashen came with her husband, Ethyn, a dental surgeon, from Brisbane far away in Australia to open a practice in the City of London she had no thought that one day she would be running a guest house in Wales. It cannot have been the rewards which attracted her. In her elegant, early Victorian villa Bron Heulog (which means *Sunshine Hill*) guests sleep luxuriously on generously mattressed brass bedsteads, canopied with lace. On the walls hang some of her husband's lifetime collection of paintings. Yet in 1987 bed and substantial breakfast cost only £8.50 and a three-course steak dinner in the elegant Regency dining room was £5. And it is the only guest house we have stayed in where guests are urged to play the grand piano.

The choice of places to stay in the Tanat range from pubs to trellised cottages with roses round the door and £8.50 was the average price for an overnight stay. The cost of dinner rarely exceed £10 and was often considerably less.

And the Valley folk are so helpful. At the Hand, former church warden John Hughes happily takes visitors on a tour of St Dogfan's parish church. It is a rewarding experience, marred only by sadness that the church's famous star ceiling has been painted over. The ceiling, which was an exact astronomical map of the heavens, was the work of a former vicar, Canon Silas Evans, an astrologer of note. It was quite awe-inspiring and for a decade one of the Valley's jewels. Alas, a successor of the Canon had the whole map painted over.

Entertainment is varied in the Valley and impressive. Mrs Eluned Davies Jones conducts Côr Dyffryn Tanat (the Tanat Valley Choir), 55 men and women whose keenness — some travel 28 miles for twice weekly rehearsals — is reflected in competition victories.

Performances in the village have included 'Elijah' and the Messiah.

Gaynor Richfield acted with Jack Hulbert and Cicely Courtnedge. Since she moved to a converted mill in the Valley she has had to give up her professional career. She has no time to follow it. Most of her days — and many of her evenings — are taken up with running the two companies, adult and junior, which make up the Tanat Theatre Club. Whilst husband Richard is away acting in TV and the live theatre Gaynor is either rehearsing an adult production in the village hall or the Youth Theatre in the old village school which the Theatre Club has just bought for rehearsal rooms and to use as a 'Little Theatre'.

One attraction that must not be missed is a lady called Olwen Edwards. Miss Edwards and a host of cats run the remarkable Plough Inn on the outskirts of the village. It is a survival, a link with a lost age of memorable topers. One of the last of the 'Jug Pubs'. For those unfortunate to be young some explanation is necessary. 'Jug Pubs' were the first inns and date back to medieval days. There are no pumps. Beer is brought from barrels in the cellar in large jugs — or, as in the nimble Miss Edwards' case, in single glasses. In the fifties, though jug pubs were rare, every country town or village had at least one. The Plough at Llanrhaeadr must be one of the few to escape the tasteless redevelopment orgies of the brewing monopolies. No ale ever tasted so good as the liquor drunk straight from the barrel. As Ian drank rather more than his share of it we listened intently to Miss Edwards' cats, spread like a hand of cards in the fireplace. The Elizabethan dramatist Webster talked of 'ale would make a cat speak'. And Ian claims he heard a welcoming feline whisper. A visit to the Plough is to participate in history. When the Plough goes, there goes with it our last link with village life in the Middle Ages.

The other wonder of Llanrhaeadr — and, indeed, officially of Wales — is Pistyll Rhaeadr. No words can prepare a visitor for his first sight of this mighty waterfall.

23

It is beyond description and sadly it was named by someone with little knowledge of Welsh. Both *pistyll* and *rhaeadr* mean waterfall. It represents the first spectacular descent of the river Disgynfa, which rises not far from Llyn Caws (*the Lake of Cheese*). Its first moorland miles take the river through ancient battle fields where Owain Gwynedd's army fought in times gone by. past the 'Hill of Graves', through the 'Place Where the Soldiers Were Caught', to the lip of the Berwyns. It is in reality two falls, which might explain its curious name. The first drops 160 feet into a pool, the wall of which, over the millenia, has been gouged out to create a gap through which the river takes its final eighty-foot leap into a pool of boiling froth. One half of this natural wonder is owned by the Squire of the Tanat, Sir Watkin Williams Wynn, the other by the Earl of Powys. It was a former Sir Watkin of enlightened vision who, in the nineteenth century, planted the hanging garden of beech and oak, larch, ash, sycamore and magnificent rowan in the cliffs on either side of the headlong water. The Falls may be visited with ease. There is a car park through the farmyard. A footbridge over the Disgynfa leads to a path which climbs up the bank to the first pool. Less hardy visitors can enjoy panoramic views of the falls in greater comfort from the verandah of a log cabin cafe overlooking the river.

Panoramic views too from the enchanting gardens at Dolwen, Cefn Coch, about a mile from Llanrhaeadr — most of it uphill. The gardens are open to the discerning public, but not to coaches which would, anyway, find it difficult negotiating the single-track lane that winds 1,000 feet up into the Berwyns. The gardens surround the idyllic cottage which Frances Denby shared with General Sir Oliver Leese until his death. Sir Oliver was one of Monty's wartime commanders and one of the few generals about whom no-one has said a bad word. In retirement he became an international authority on cacti and Japanese bonsai treatment. When he died most of his collection of cacti went to the Royal Horticultural Society's gardens at

Wisley. Some remain. Here and there in this garden of heavenly delights miniature trees grow in scaled down settings. For the rest, the garden is bold. A place of lakes and waterfalls, of sweeping flower beds and massive boulders, guarding shrubs.

It is a garden of unbounded interest. By the banks of the stream stands a stone temple lantern which Sir Oliver brought from Japan and below it the sculpted figure of a young girl bends over the water to dip her hand. It is the work of Frances' daughter, Philippa. The garden stretches over six acres yet it remains essentially a cottage garden. It looks as though it has existed for centuries yet fifteen years ago it was a wasteland of scrub and bramble. There are still firm traces of the General's boundless good humour. He was president of the M.C.C. Over the summerhouse is a copy of the famous Lords Father Time weathercock. In the conservatory Frances has preserved his Doll's House. His love of the miniature went far beyond bonsai. The house is crammed with miniature furniture and tiny people.

The garden is fascinating but quite the finest thing about it is its owner Frances Denby. A lady greatly loved, merry as Christmas, she keeps the garden weed-free and well fed with the help of only one man, her gardener David Cotterill, and her neighbour's horse which provides the manure.

Mrs Denby is a great conservationist in a valley where there is much to preserve. People have lived here since the Stone Age. Romans mined the lead and there remains on one farm a stretch of Roman pavement whilst at another, Glaniwrch, spindles from the Stone Age have been found among Roman artefacts.

The most pleasing survival from our ancient past is a meadow on the Bitfel Rare Breeds Farm at Cefn Coch. It has not been cultivated for 700 years and in consequence over fifty separate species of native flora grow. The Rare Breeds farm of which it is a part is run by Mrs Jenny Meredith. Her stock includes thirty varieties of poultry, rare geese and duck and twenty different rare breeds of sheep, goats, pigs and cattle. Most of the stock is hand-tamed and the whole farm is a children's paradise.

One of the most attractive aspects of the Tanat as a holiday centre is a facility which unhappily is rare in the outside world. Pets are welcome at most hotels and guest houses. One, Gegin Fedw, at Pen-y-garnedd, even offers 'Bed and Breakfast for Horses'.

This magic valley and its surroundings constantly surprises. Llanfyllin's claim to fame in earlier days was that it produced so many drunkards it provoked the aphorism 'Old ale fills Llanfyllin with young widows'. It has an altogether more charming story of love and marriage.

During the Napoleonic Wars French prisoners were captured in such numbers that the Government ran out of prisons to hold them. Certain officers were paroled to live in civilian homes. Some came to Llanfyllin, and among them was a young infantry lieutenant, Pierre Augeraud. He had been captured with his regiment, the 5th Infantry, during the Peninsula Campaign when Wellington laid siege to the Spanish town of Badajos. In Llanfyllin he was quartered on the first floor of the town's Council House.

Desperately lonely he began a series of mural paintings on the walls of his billet. They are haunting, melancholy pictures of a fairyland far away. In all there are twelve of these pictures and they cover every wall of the sitting room over what is now Llanfyllin Drug Store. Artistically they are romantic rather than competent. They show a wild landscape of gothic crags and dark seas and they all have one feature in common. In every one an angler, in the uniform of a Napoleonic soldier, sits fishing. Always alone. Though they are not well drawn the paintings have a deep sadness that comes across the centuries. Yet the story has a happy ending. As he sat in his window watching people in the main street below he saw in the churchyard opposite the pretty daughter of the Rector of Llanfyllin. In church, whilst her father was preaching, he made surreptitious drawings of the girl. At last they met and fell in love.

When the rector, the Rev. William Williams, heard of this he was furious. He had preached against the evil of Napoleon from his pulpit and he was aghast that his own daughter should be fraternising with the enemy. He appealed to Lt. General Sir Rowland Hill, a distinguished Peninsula commander, and as a result the luckless lieutenant was repatriated to France.

Augeraud returned to Llanfyllin after the war ended. The Rector was dead, his widow sympathetic and at last the couple were married. To live, one hopes, happily ever after. The present owners of the Council House (the Drug Store), Suart and Clare Danby, are delighted to welcome visitors but it is essential to telephone first.

Another amateur artist, though one with considerably more skill than the French lieutenant, was the Reverend John Parker, Vicar of St Michael the Archangel, Llanyblodwel, between 1845 and 1860. A splendidly eccentric man of means, he spent the last sixteen years of his life turning this simple border church into a High Gothic, happily exuberant feast of colour. Scriptural quotations in gothic script embellish the walls which glow with bright colour. He virtually rebuilt the church. The ceiling of the nave he put in is modelled on St David's Cathedral, the brilliant decoration based on the crypt at Winchester. He designed the church seating, including a double-decker pulpit. The arches of the windows in the nave were gilded with gold leaf, but the pride and joy of the Rev. Parker was the unique spire he designed and built. It is octagonal in shape and its creation gave him many headaches. In his diary he wrote:

> 'Jan 2, 1856: Yesterday and today I have been trying to strike the curve intended for the sides of my spire. It is very difficult. I have not yet succeeded...'

27

When he wasn't working on his church the Rev. Parker was painting in water colours in the mountains. He was a much-loved man and a generous one. He gave dinners to the local men who worked on the church and met all the costs of rebuilding the church out of his own pocket.

Churlishly a successor had all the Rev. Parker's work covered by whitewash and for sixty years it remained hidden. Thankfully in 1960 an enlightened Diocesan Advisory Committee began the unusual task of restoring a restoration. Today, thanks to those men, the little church is once again glowing with colour.

Llanyblodwel is a village alive to the call of tradition. From the reign of Henry VIII until the 1920s the same family held the licence of the Wheatsheaf Inn on the banks of the Tanat, where, incidentally, there is half a mile of fly fishing available for trout and grayling at £2.50 a day. The Tanat, as anglers will know, is especially famous for its grayling.

It was in the Tanat Valley at Sycharth that Owain Glyndŵr had his great wooden palace. The Welsh gentry were permitted only wood for their houses because, though stone walls may not a prison make, they do make effective fortifications. The size of the mound on which Owain's house was built is an indication of the dimensions of the palace. No trace of the buildings remain but we do have a contemporary description. It was written by Glyndŵr's bard, Iolo Goch:

> 'Tis water girdled wide about
> It shows a wide and stately door
> Reached by a bridge the water o'er.
> 'Tis formed of buildings coupled fair
> Coupled is every couple there
> Within a quadrate structure tall
> Muster the merry pleasures all.
> Co-jointly are the angles bound
> No flaw in all the place is found.

Structures in contact meet the eye
Upon the hillocks top on high
Into each other fastened they
The form of a hard knot display.
There dwells the chief we all extol
In timber house on lightsome knoll.
Upon four wooden columns proud
Each column thick and firmly based
And upon each a loft is placed...

A descendant of Owain Glyndŵr still lives nearby at Llangedwyn. He is Sir Watkin Williams Wynn, the present baronet, a vividly eighteenth century personality, who, like Glyndŵr, is a former professional soldier. The family has many distinctions, including having a delicious pudding named in its honour.

The Watkin Williams Wynn Family Pudding dates back to the late eighteenth century. It is unique in using bone marrow in place of suet. Here is the recipe:

Mix 4 oz of finely chopped or grated beef marrow, 4 oz sugar, 4 oz soft white breadcrumbs, the strained juice and finely grated rind of a lemon. Stir in the well beaten yolks of two eggs, followed by the whites *very* stiffly mixed. Scrape and spoon into a well-buttered pudding basin, filling to the three-quarter mark. Cover with well-buttered kitchen foil, place in a pan of boiling water and boil it for two hours, topping up with boiling water as necessary. Tip onto a hot plate and pour hot raspberry jam before serving.

More soberly, it was at Llangedwyn Hall that Bishop Heber wrote his evening hymn 'God who madest earth and heaven' after hearing an old harpist play the Welsh tune 'Ar hyd y nos'.

Just by the Hall gates is the charming parish church of St Cedwyn with a well preserved fourteenth century effigy of a village priest and some enviable pre-Raphaelite glass.

In 1987 the Tanat had an especial cause for pride. For the first time since it was founded in 1966 a British player won the Suntory World Match Play Golf Championship at Wentworth.

He is a farmer's son, Ian Woosnam, and he trained at Llanymynech golf course overlooking the valley. The course has one other claim to fame which is surely unique. It spreads across two countries. Fifteen of its holes are in Wales, the other three in England.

Between Llangedwyn and Llanrhaeadr, on the high road to Bala, there is a curious 11 ft high standing stone, 'Post y Wiber', which means the post of the winged serpent. According to a local tale the neighbourhood was being terrified by just such a dragon. To rid themselves of it villagers draped the stone with a red cross and the serpent, thinking it to be a rival serpent, charged it and killed itself.

Happier traditions, the crafts of the countryside, are being carried out in delightful surroundings at Llangedwyn Mill. The mill itself houses a museum showing the traditional crafts and life in the valleys over the centuries and there are in addition a cafe, a shop, a children's play area and twelve craft workshops, all on the Tanat banks.

How to leave this truly happy valley? The most satisfying way is after a lavish Welsh tea at the Glyndŵr Tea Rooms in Penybontfawr where everything is homemade — including the tea rooms. Leave the cafe and turn right for Lake Vyrnwy just opposite the man who is making rocking horses on the pavement. Do stop for a chat. He is a delightful man named Bill Shorto, a magician, authority on fairies and a talented woodcarver. Under the saddle cloths of his rocking horses, all called Merlin, is a tiny cavity into which Bill puts copies of his favourite poem.

A final warning. Do not take the Vyrnwy road if you have no head for heights. The 14-mile drive round the lake is enchanting but the road from there to Bala or the other one to Dinas Mawddwy are hair-raising, single track roads. The views are magnificent, of course. But it's another road that is not for the faint-hearted. Ian was much happier on the charming switchback road from Llangedwyn to Oswestry, a mere 10 miles away. But whichever road you take it will not be easy saying au revoir to the Tanat. No-one ever says goodbye.

The Ceiriog Valley

Photo: Wales Tourist Board

THE CEIRIOG AND CHIRK

The entrance to the Ceiriog Valley is dominated by Chirk aqueduct, one of the many great works in Wales by Thomas Telford, an engineering genius whom the poet Southey wittily dubbed the Colossus of Roads. The aqueduct has ten spans of forty feet each which carry the Shropshire Union canal seventy feet above the River Ceiriog. When it reaches land this river in the sky plunges through a tunnel which was the first to have a towing path going through its length. Until Telford's tunnel barges had to be "legged" by boatmen who lay on their sides and pushed with their feet against the tunnel walls. The tunnel was built so that the barges would not spoil the view for the family at Chirk Castle.

The foundation stone for the aqueduct was laid on 17 June, 1796. Only five years later it opened for business. Today, nearly two centuries later, the cast iron plates which made the trough — another innovation, until then canal troughs were lined with puddled clay — are still in use. Running alongside the aqueduct is a railway viaduct made of brick and stone which took only four years to build. The viaduct is 286 yards long and 100 feet high. It comprises ten 45 ft arches and it was the work of Henry Robertson who also designed and built the Whitehurst Viaduct across the Dee.

Faced with these modern tributes to the ingenuity of man, we thought it would do us no harm to visit the twelfth century parish church. It proved a delightful contrast. The church has interesting monuments to the Myddeltons of

Chirk whose home, Chirk Castle, is the spectacular guardian of the valley.

Chirk Castle crouches on its hill at the mouth of the Ceiriog valley like a stone toad, menacing and watchful. Though much altered over the centuries it still remains, from the outside at least, a border fortress built for war and domination.

When we drove up through the magnificent eighteenth century gates, made by two local brothers Robert and John Davies of Bersham, we thought that the first view of the castle could not have changed greatly since Owain Glyndŵr saw it as a seven-year-old boy over five hundred years ago. For him it was the end of a long journey from his home in the Tanat, down the Ceiriog, before his horse rattled over the drawbridge into the castle courtyard.

Scarcely changed at all is the chapel where he prayed morning and night with his fellow servants and his guardians, the Arundels. It was in this chapel that after an all-night vigil he was presented with a consecrated sword, admitted esquire and began his long military training. A training which was to stand him in good stead subsequently fighting his Arundel patron. There is little sign of change either in the Adams Tower, or "Constable's Tower", as it was known in Owain's day. The grim dungeon, in the castle's foundations, has little light and no ventilation. That was for the poor. French knights captured at Agincourt in 1415 were worth considerable sums in ransom money and were treated accordingly. They were kept for six years in the Lower Guard chamber above the dungeon, which has a fireplace and an efficient ventilation system.

The Myddeltons were hospitable even to their prisoners. As that great eighteenth century traveller Thomas Pennant quaintly remarks: "... the dungeon must not be forgotten. The descent is by forty-two steps but according to the laudable usage of the present lord, the captives endure but a short and easy confinement; and even that passes imperceptibly, amidst the good cheer and generous liquors bestowed on them by the kind warder to whose custody they are committed."

Chirk has had many owners. From the Mortimers who built it to their successors the Earls of Arundel, the names are a roll-call of Britain's most powerful warrior families: the Mowbrays, the Beauchamps, the Beauforts, the Stanleys, and Elizabeth I's favourite, the Earl of Leicester.

In 1595 Chirk went to a merchant adventurer, Thomas Myddelton, whose family owned it until 1978 when it was bought for the nation. Now it is owned and has been extensively restored by the National Trust.

During the Civil War its then owner Sir Thomas Myddelton was a distinguished commander on both sides in turn and twice saw his home captured and partially demolished.

Celia, who has no interest in wars and warriors, preferred the State Rooms, which, with the drawing room and gallery, were restored at the time of Charles II's Restoration and contain fine furniture. We were both riveted by a humble wooden water pipe. It was part of London's first fresh water supply system, a 38-mile pipe line engineered between the city and the Chadwell and Amwell springs in Essex by Sir Hugh Myddelton of Chirk and financed with the profits from his lead mines in North Wales.

Besides the furniture there are many fine tapestries and paintings. We have two favourites. One in the splendid Servants' Hall is indifferently done. When it was painted in January 1729 by an artist called Whitmore he was paid two guineas. It shows "a poor deformed cripple, taken into the family by Sir Richard Myddelton and kept for charity from his youth until his death." He was given no work apparently. But he was given a courtesy title. He was "The Ornament of the Kitchens".

We also relished a landscape "Llanrhaiadr Falls", painted by Richard Wilson, the "Father" of English landscape painting. According to the story, as he finished his work one of those annoying onlookers who plague painters suggested the picture would be improved with some "sheeps". With delightful perversity — and no doubt intentional misunderstanding — Wilson did exactly as he was asked. Or nearly so. Look at the foot of the falls. Ships?

Out in the car park, running in a line from the Home Farm to the lake, is the track of the most extraordinary memorial to the Dark Ages in Britain, Offa's Dyke. The Dyke is a massive earthwork, built in the eighth century by King Offa the Angle to mark the borders between his kingdom and Wales.

Offa's Dyke has been overtaken by technology. Most of it has been swallowed up by the Offa's Dyke Path, a 160-mile ramble from the River Severn, over the Clwydian Range, to Bodfari, finally reaching the sea at Prestatyn. We have been told the walk is a marvellous experience and a testing one but have felt no desire to confirm this view. Anyone who does should remember it is stiff walking and should not be attempted without maps, boots, a compass and rain gear. From Chirk the Dyke Path crosses the Pontcysyllte aqueduct — not the best place for those, like Ian, with no head for heights — passes through Llangollen, continues to the Eglwyseg Rocks and beyond them over the Llandegla moors and the Clwydians before finally dropping to "earth" at Bodfari.

It was near here at Brynkynallt that the great Duke of Wellington suffered one of his few defeats. He was thrashed in a stand-up fight — by a girl. It happened during a boyhood visit to his grandmother, Viscountess Dungannon, who lived there. Wellington and the girl's brother were playing marbles and an argument developed. The girl intervened and had him running.

The valleys of Glyndŵr Country are almost without exception wide and fertile. The exception is to be found in the first miles of the valley of the Ceiriog. The hills rise steeply from the river bank into cliffs of bare rock above great acres of woodland. It is called the "Switzerland of Wales" and in Owain's day it was the haunt of a notable outlaw, Gruffydd ap Dafydd ap Gruffydd. A bold, charismatic figure, there exists in the National Archive a letter he wrote to Owain's enemy Lord Grey, who, Gruffydd claimed, had tried to ambush him at a time when he was under safe conduct to negotiate a pardon.

Gruffydd writes with spendid anger: "I was told that you are in purpose to let your men burn and slay in any land which succours me and in which I am taken. Without doubt as many men as you slay for my sake and as many houses as you burn for my sake as many will I burn and slay for yours. And doubt not that I will have bread and ale of the best that is in your lordship."

Curiously Grey chose to respond in verse. He wrote:
"We hope we shall do you a privy thing
A rope, a ladder and a ring
High on the gallows for to swing
And this shall be your ending..."

Inhabitants of the Ceiriog Valley are every bit as independent to this day, though they are much kinder to visitors. The valley abounds in hotels, inns, guest houses and private houses where bed and breakfast will cost far less than lunch in most cities.

In Glyn Ceiriog there are two hotels, the Glyn Valley and Plas Owen, and two cosy, seventeenth century inns, the Royal Oak and in the countryside nearby, the Golden Pheasant. We chose the Pheasant which combines the friendly ambience of a bar parlour with the cuisine and appointments of a luxury hotel. It has been owned and run by the same family for nearly half a century. In its early days it was the village brewery. It has shooting rights and a stretch of the river and is surrounded by delightful gardens. Jenny Gibourg, whose father bought the Pheasant, runs it now. She is a talented designer. Every bedroom differs from its neighbour. There are suites with triangular baths, four-poster beds — one dating back to the seventeenth century — and in one room is a splendid Victorian bed of mahogany. The decor in the residents' lounge is Victorian, the cocktail bar is Chinese

Chippendale and has what the vivacious Jenny insists is the best view of the valley. Her sister Jane Rushworth makes the same claim for the view from the Riding Centre she runs a little way up the road.

One very curious thing about the Ceiriog hotels and guest houses is that everyone seems to have an aviary. There are, fittingly, golden pheasants at the Golden Pheasant but Jane Rushworth not only has an aviary; she keeps chipmunks, marmosets and Jasper and Bandit, a pair of racoons. Along with the 34 horses they are great favourites with the children who flock there every summer, unaccompanied, for riding holidays, which often include two-day trail rides in the hills with frequent stops for delicious picnics. When the children tire of animals they go down to the workshop where husband Mike, a cabinet maker, makes exquisite bespoke furniture. He also built the heated swimming pool, and the ranch-style dormitory, dug the trout pool for adolescent anglers and laid the cross country course.

There is a strong tradition of wood-carving in the Ceiriog. At Ceiriog Crafts Theo Davies carved two Olympic Hockey trophies for the landlord of the Glyn Valley, John Cranwell, at the time manager of the British Hockey team. Theo used six different timbers and completed the job in a week. He carves bardic chairs and furniture to order. A coffee table he made for a board room had two hundred and twelve different pieces of wood inlaid into the surface. He has also restored much of the wood carving at Plas Newydd, home in the eighteenth century of the Ladies of Llangollen. But the work which gives him the greatest pleasure is making aids for sick people. It all began when he designed a "one off" standing frame, complete with small table, for a paralysed girl patient at the Orthopaedic Hospital at Gobowen across the border in Shropshire. The frame stands on four legs with supports for the body and a hand-rail. It was such a success that Theo is now making ten a week. When we visited him he was going into production with his latest invention, a rocking stool which restores the sense of balance in people who have suffered from seizures. He designed it with the help of a physiotherapist who is delighted with the result.

Across the road at "Frondeg", John Garnet spins and his wife Joyce weaves. Joyce is the boss and John doesn't mind a bit. He was a director of a large company in Birmingham until he was made redundant in his early fifties. Joyce was a crafts teacher and a creative weaver — so he went to work for his wife. They opened a craft centre in Birmingham, then decided to get nearer to the raw materials. Now they give classes for visitors. John spins the fleece of local sheep and Joyce turns it into stylish garments.

At Pontfadog take the road to Bronygarth where, in 1165, Henry II's invading English army was defeated by Owain Gwynedd, one of the greatest Welsh princes.

The battle of Crogen represented Henry II's most ambitious campaign to conquer Wales. He assembled a huge army at Oswestry while Owain Gwynedd summoned his chieftains to Corwen. Henry marched towards them but was soon halted by the impenetrable forest which in those days covered the valley floor. He sent his foresters forward to hack a way through for the army and ordered them to be guarded by the flower of his army and his pikemen.

They were ambushed at Bronygarth by advance troops from the Welsh army. The king had a narrow escape from death, Hubert de Clare putting his own body in the path of an arrow aimed at the sovereign, and though the troops managed to fight their way to the peaks of the Berwyns they had lost so many men that the king was forced to retreat. In revenge he had the eyes torn out of the head of Owain Gwynedd's son whom he was holding as a hostage. The English soldiers were so impressed by the fighting qualities of their opponents that for many years after the battle the English word for courage was "crogen".

The valley boasts three poets, Huw Morus, of whom

more later, the Eisteddfod-winning bard the Rev. Robert Ellis and Ceiriog Hughes who was described as the Welsh Robert Burns. This happy conjunction is celebrated by the Ceiriog Memorial Institute which was built to honour the three poets and Thomas Jefferson, who was of Welsh descent. The Institute also houses the magistrates court, a small library and an idiosyncratic museum of local objects which include bronze age spindles, minute bibles and fearsome medieval weapons; a small replica of King Arthur's round table and the only statue of Owain Glyndŵr in the whole of Glyndŵr Country. Indeed it is the only statue of the great Welsh hero either of us can remember having seen outside Cardiff. His presence there is puzzling since the only time he visited the Welsh capital was when he burnt it down.

Not far away a happy morning can be spent wandering round the Trout Farm at Glyn Ceiriog which carries the singular advertising slogan, "Why stay at home and be insulted when you can just as easily be offended at Upper Mills Trout Farm?" So compelling was the notion that when we went to buy a brace of fish for supper we felt curiously let down at the friendly reception.

There is game fishing along the 18-mile length of the valley, both in the river and in well-stocked trout pools for the novice angler. Good shooting too at Llanarmon, Nantyr and Chirk. There are countless miles of walking amidst the breath-taking scenery of the Berwyn mountains and Cader Fronwen or, to the south, by the tributaries of the Vyrnwy and the Severn, named for Sabrina, an ancient British king's daughter who was drowned by her jealous step-mother. Like most of Glyndŵr Country it is relatively undiscovered by holiday-makers who drive down the A5 past these hidden valleys heading for the crowded coast. Walk into the hills through the Ceiriog Forest with its charming picnic site at Plas Nantir, and you arrive on moors where you might never see another person all day.

But if it does seem to you that the valley offers nothing but fishing, shooting, riding and walking it would be as well not to say so in the presence of Brian James who, with his wife Angela, owns and runs the valley's greatest tourist attraction, the Chwarel Wynne Slate Mines.

He was so incensed at the charge that he compiled this list of some of the valley's more bizarre attractions (see page opposite for map) which he very kindly agreed to let us print.

1. Chirk Aqueduct, built by Thomas Telford to carry the Shropshire Union Canal over the Ceiriog Valley. 230 yards long, 75 feet high. Work started in 1796 and finished in 1801. The tunnel, constructed at the same time, was not necessary but the owners of Chirk Castle were unwilling to have their views obstructed by the banks of the canal.

2. Chirk Castle, built by Roger Mortimer in 1298 on the site of a much earlier motte and bailey, took 16 years to build. It saw much fighting during the Civil War of 1654-1660. The world-famous wrought iron gates at the entrance to the park were made in 1719 by the Davies Brothers of Bersham.

3. A replica of Stonehenge — A Victorian folly erected for Francis West, owner of the Quinta estate.

4. The Lime Kilns at Bronygarth, used between 1770 and 1920. The lime used in the construction of Chirk Aqueduct came from here.

5. Castle Mill. The cottages now here formed part of a corn mill dating from 1365. The Battle of Crogen is also reputed to have been fought here — Henry II's troops were harried by Welsh querrillas led by Owain Gwynedd in 1165.

6. Offa's Dyke. Raised by Offa, King of Mercia, in 776 A.D. to separate the warring tribes of England and Wales. Runs for 173 miles from the north to south coasts of Wales.

7. The Gap of the Dead (Adwy'r Beddau). A break in the Dyke close to Castle Mill is were the dead of

Henry II's army were buried after the battle of Crogen.

8. Gypsy Corner — so called after Gypsy Smith, who lived for a number of years in the cave at the foot of the quarry on the north side of the road. He lived by making clothes pegs and tap dancing for beer money in the local hostelries.

9. Herber Gate, once a Toll House, this part of the B4500 was a privately owned turnpike in 1863.

10. Tan y Garth Hall. Built as a hunting lodge at the end of the 19th century for the Tuan Muda of Sarawak (Brooke the White Rajah).

11. Oldest and largest oak tree in Wales at Pontfadog — once a bull was trapped in its hollow trunk, sic Guinness Book of Records.

12. Cheshire Home — once the Queen's Hotel. Lloyd George, Ellen Terry and many other notables stayed here. Iron tramway bridge (see number 17) may be seen in the grounds.

13. Stone 'wheel', located high in the hillside at Bryn Bugeilin, may have been a mill stone. Although 'bugeilin' indicates connections with sheep farming (*bugail* — a shepherd). A mound containing a burial urn was excavated here some years ago.

14. Standing stone, *carreg y bug,* 9 feet high. Local legend suggests that it marks the grave of a giant of many years past — probably a boundary marker.

15. Upper and Berwyn woollen mills. Last remains of the thriving woollen industry worked by water power from 1810 to 1951. One is now a craft workshop, the other a trout farm.

16. The Ceiriog Institute — a Museum Library, meeting place and courtroom, built in 1911 by subscription in memory of the famous valley poets Huw Morus, Ceiriog Hughes and Cynddelw.

17. Glyn Valley Tramway engine shed and station — all that remains of the narrow guage railway constructed in 1873 to carry the minerals and woollen

goods produced in the valley to Telford's canal at Chirk — also carried passengers. Closed 1935. Part of the Tramway further up the valley was presented to the National Trust and forms a pleasant walk.

18. Chwarel Wynne, one of a number of slate quarries in the valley — quarrying was the major employment of the valley. Chwarel Wynne was worked from 1750 to 1928. Now open as a Museum.

19. Carved fireplace in the Glyn valley Hotel. Carries a biblical inscription in Gaelic.

20. Hafod y Gynfawr. Tudor residence in the village. Cromwell's troops were supposed to have been billeted here during the Civil War.

21. Pandy Caves. A former granite mine, now flooded. Worked from 1895 to 1905.

22. Pandy Crag, a high outcrop. Quarried for its deposits of chinastone and much used by climbers.

23. Pandy Mill, believed to be the first fulling mill in Wales and dating from 1365.

24. Pontymeibion. Birthplace of the poet Huw Morus. A royalist, his anti-puritan verse made him famous. A stone seat used by him has been moved from its original roadside vantage point to the garden of the farmhouse, Erw Gerrig.

25. The Hendre 'Granite' Quarry. Worked from 1875 to 1950, producing road stone from deposits of volcanic ash. Originally deposits of the rock were found when digging the mill stream for a gunpowder mill working here between 1870 and 1879.

26. Tomen y meirw (Tomb of the Dead). Ancient burial mound. Unauthorised excavation is supposed to have led to the discovery of a human skull with red hair still attached to it.

27. Tomen y Gwyddel (Tomb of the Irishman). Ancient burial mound.

28. Hafod Adams. Reputedly the oldest house in the valley. Supposed to have ecclesiastical connections.

The field opposite was known in Welsh as the field of the graves.

29. Ffordd Saeson — the English Road. Ancient trackway supposed to have been used by Henry II's defeated troops in 1165.

30. Cae Cerrig Gwynion — the Fort of the White Stones. Ancient hill fort reputedly used later by Henry II's defeated troops in 1165.

31. Penybryn. White-washed farmhouse overlooking Llanarmon. Birthplace of Wales' most famous poet, John Ceiriog Hughes.

32. Churchyard mound may have been used as a pulpit by the church's patron saint, Germanus. Two pulpits.

33. Dolwen. An ancient farmhouse reputedly used by Owain Glyndŵr, but famous more recently for possession of the first W.C. in Wales.

34. Sarphle. Site of a find of over 500 Roman silver coins.

35. The Falls of Ceiriog — a series of small water falls near the source of the River Ceiriog.

36. The Ceiriog Forest, a vast acreage of Forestry Commission woodland offering an attractive picnic and walking area.

Brian's own contribution to the places of interest, Chwarel Wynne, is a fascinating piece of industrial history. There are no fairies at the bottom of the James' garden but there are thirty assorted peacocks and hens, a nature trail and three and a half miles of galleries and underground slate workings in a hillside that has been quarried since the ninth century. Serious quarrying did not begin until the mid-eighteenth century when Chwarel Wynne was an open-cast quarry owned by Edward Wynne of New Hall, Glyn Ceiriog. In 1861 the quarry was bought by a consortium of wealthy landowners. Unlike the quarries in the Tanat Valley, the Ceiriog quarries had a water outlet, the Ellesmere canal. A tramway linked quarry and canal and eventually the line was extended to meet the Great Western railway.

The quarry was financed in its heyday in the late nineteenth and early twentieth centuries by money made from railways. A family called Rooper made huge profits out of what was to become Watford Junction and then very sensibly ran for the Welsh hills.

The James's live in the villa the Roopers built within walking distance of their quarry. It is a handsome house but the Jameses are from time to time uneasy. The Roopers, blissfully disregarding the laws of gravity, built the house on a slate tip.

Says Brian: "Only the front porch prevents the house from slipping into the valley."

He is a former London publicist who, like the Roopers, headed for the Welsh hills when he worked out one day he was spending a thousand pounds a year commuting to a job he didn't much enjoy. He has a great admiration for the second generation of Roopers.

"Name was George and by the standards of his day he was a very benevolent boss. He supplied the village below with free electricity and water. There was no child labour here. No-one under the age of 16 was allowed underground."

Not over-benevolent we thought. The boom-time when the quarries were most profitable was in the early days of the twentieth century. Seventy-seven men produced 2,000 tons of workable slate in a single year. They did it by smashing at the rock face with an iron bar and with explosives they had to buy, working by the light of candles they also had to buy at the company shop. Though their wages were pitifully small, injured workers had to pay 8d. for medical attention. The doctor only charged 6d. but the company took a two-penny profit on every injured man.

When the James's bought the house they had no idea of opening the mine to the public but Brian's private fascination grew until it became an obsession.

He recalls: "We began by opening the workings and

45

making a museum of the relics we found in them. When the mine closed in 1946 the men had just dropped their tools and walked out. In the manager's desk, for example, there were the complete records of the mine going back nearly a hundred years."

Visitors now — up to 20,000 a year, including annual tours by eleven schools — reach the mine via a nature trail, a fascinating ramble. Birds abound and it's difficult to believe that under the flowers and ferns and the trees are the tips of thousands of tons of waste, dug out to get to the comparatively small percentage of slate. The mine itself is well worth a visit. Tableaux of working miners vividly show the horrendous working conditions and the commentary by our guide was inspired.

As you leave the mine do pay a visit to the Glyn Valley Hotel at the bottom of the hill, either to book into the sumptuous honeymoon suite with a four-poster bed or, as we did, to see the fascinating collection of photographs of the old Ceiriog Valley Tramway. Marvellous archive material. The Tramway Station used to be next door to the hotel. Alas the railway no longer runs but there is a consolation. The old track is now a lovely nature trail. It specially pleased Ian, who is almost as broad as he is long. Unlike most of the many splendid walks which abound in the valley, it is "on the flat". Entrances to the trail are well signed.

As we drove further up the valley a military band on the car radio was playing "Men of Harlech". It was an eerie coincidence. The words of that stirring march were written by the Ceiriog poet, Ceiriog Hughes, and we were on our way to the home of an earlier writer of those stirring ballads this valley inspires, written in the seventeenth century in support of Charles I. So stirring indeed that Cromwell sent a detachment of troops to silence him.

The poet was Huw Morus.

He was a farmer's son. Born in 1622 at Pontymeibion, now a pony-trekking centre, and apprenticed much against his will to a tanner of hides, he was by all accounts a dissolute youth and lazy. Yet before he was thirty he was already the most famous poet in Wales. He lived until he was 84, through six reigns, and his principles never wavered. When Charles I was executed he wrote a series of witty lampoons on Cromwell. When Charles II regained the throne Morus, the Ceiriog Nightingale as he was known, wrote a bitterly ironic "Lamentation to Oliver's Men". He was loyal to Charles' successor James II until he tried to smash the Church of England, whereupon Huw wrote songs in support of the Prince of Orange. He was held in high respect by his neighbours. In his day the clergyman left the church first, followed by the congregation in order of social importance. When Morus went to church on Sunday the clergyman insisted on leaving the church after him.

He lived for many years at Erw Gerrig (the stony acre), the sixteenth century farmhouse owned by his brother. On his death bed he is said to have written:

> "Now to my rest I hurry away
> To the world which lasts for ever and aye
> To paradise this beautiful place
> Trusting alone in the Lord of Grace."

When George Borrow came to the Ceiriog he made a beeline for the poet's birthplace, Pontymeibion, which his guide told him meant the bridge of the children. The village of Pandy, which he passed on the way, was the site of the first fulling mill in Wales. Borrow scarcely gave it a second thought. He wanted to sit in Huw Morus' chair, a slate bench with a high back, set into the hill, with the initials H.M.B. (Huw Morus Bard). It took him a long time and a heated struggle with brambles and wild shrubs to reach it. We didn't anticipate any trouble because the chair is now set into a wall in the garden of Erw Gerrig where it commands a view over the Ceiriog that we like to think would have brought a poem to old Huw's lips.

Indeed we like to think that if he could come back he

would write a poem about the very remarkable lady who lives in his old home.

When Anne Kynaston came to Erw Gerrig it was a ruin. There were, in fact, eighty-eight stony acres; the farmhouse and its outbuildings were derelict. The livestock bought in with the farm included fifty ewes and cattle scattered about the valley. Tending them meant a daily journey of thirty miles. Her two sons were away at university, she was on her own and there was no-one in the valley who believed she would make it even through the first winter. There was no roof on the house and the wild Ceiriog winter meant there could be no attempt at re-roofing made before spring. That winter Mrs Kynaston lived under tarpaulin and she covered the roofless byres with more so that there would be shelter for the cows and their calves. There was no sanitation, no water and no electric light for months.

The first Christmas Mrs Kynaston sat with her back against crumbling walls, in a room without a floor, warming herself from a fire in a bucket and looking at a Christmas tree on a bench in a corner of the room wondering how her two sons would react to spending Christmas in a hovel. Not for the first time she was grateful for her Christian faith and relied on it to get her through. The sons reacted by pitching in to rebuilding the house, shifting tons of rubble and recruiting university friends to help. Other students helped in fields on the mountain top, hand-weeding turnip rows.

Her persistence began to pay off. A spring of delicious, pure mountain water was found and fed into a 2,000-gallon tank. Two miles of boundary fencing was erected; a local contractor began ploughing and re-sewing the land. Mrs Kynaston planted 6,000 fir trees to cover two unsightly acres of stone and rock, creating a wind break and encouraging wildlife. Unbelievably she succeeded. Within three years of moving in, the stock of ewes had grown to 200 sheep and lambs and there was now a herd of thirty cattle.

Most people would have thought it as time for a rest. Mrs Kynaston doesn't do that sort of thing. She sold off the farm and all the land except the house and fourteen acres, enrolled on a catering course, got a City and Guilds certificate and went into the farmhouse holiday business.

No-one will need to be told it was also a success. Nor that it wasn't enough to keep Mrs Kynaston busy. She decided to convert the farmhouse outbuildings into three holiday cottages with a Bardic Centre in honour of Huw Morus. Anyone who has ever tried to convert one cottage knows what a nightmare of committees, site meetings and finance meetings that can be. Almost single-handed Mrs Kynaston succeeded. Succeeded? When they were finished she won a Countryside Commission Caretaker Award. The end result is sheer bliss. There is trout fishing free to guests on her stretch of the Ceiriog and Mrs Kynaston also owns an island in the river which she lets out as a camping ground to selected scout troops. Every night a poem called supper is created on the kitchen cooker.

The first verse might be a savoury crepe or melon marinaded in liqueur; the second game pie or fresh Ceiriog trout, stuffed with prawns, and the third a pineapple cheesecake with fresh cream. Afternoon cream teas with jam and scones are also the guests to command. Dogs are welcome. There are three guest bedrooms in the house and the self-catering cottages are centrally heated and luxuriously carpeted. Each has a fully fitted kitchen/dinning room, a TV lounge with a double-bedded settee, a toilet and shower room. Two of the cottages have family bedrooms, the third has two twin-bedded rooms. And you can still go to the farmhouse for supper.

From Huw Morus' old home the view across, down or up the valley is lovely in bright spring and golden autumn. The road falls sheer to the river meadows and the water glisters between the trunks of old trees. It seems incomprehensible that there was a plan before parliament in 1924 to turn the valley into a reservoir to supply water for Warrington. There were to be two dams. One above

49

Hendre and a second upstream. The scheme would have flooded 45 farms, 37 houses and 19 other buildings. They owe their continued existence to Lloyd George who spoke against the bill before it was defeated at a second reading.

"Why should they pick out this exquisite little valley of the Ceiriog?" he asked. Why, indeed?

The gem in the heart of the Ceiriog Valley is the village of Llanarmon Dyffryn Ceiriog which is crossed by the old drovers' road. We arrived on the day that the parish church of St Garmon was dressed for the Harvest Festival. In the graveyard there is a mound on which, it is said, St Garmon preached but which almost certainly dates back to prehistoric times and the burial of a pagan prince. This sense of ancient place, this quiet continuity, is evident in the church itself. It is unremarkable save for its double pulpit and the curious bell tower, but we noticed the roll of the vicars, unbroken since the fourteenth century, and the offerings of bread and salt and coal and fruit and flowers. Such flowers. Crysanthemums glowing like flames against the washed walls; all the flowers of the season filling the little church and the altar looking like a Dutch floral painting. It was a fitting introduction to Llanarmon which, at every season from early spring to early winter is a village of flowers. In beds and borders, tubs and trays; in hanging baskets and oil drums, in wheelbarrows and butter churns; in chimney pots and plant pots, there are flowers to the left of you, flowers to the right of you, flowers at the foot of the little craft centre in what was once a mill. Beware of letting a local put a flower behind your ear or in your buttonhole. So palpably green-fingered are they that it would certainly take root.

And that perfect accompaniment to the shy and showy beauty of flowers, the sound of water. At the side of the Hand Hotel a miniature waterfall, a bonsai Pistyll; in front of the West Arms the gurglings of the infant Ceiriog. There are benches to sit on outside the Hand and across at the West you can sit, as centuries ago the drovers did, in the porch entrance.

We are always glad of these benches because it is nice to wrestle with a dilemma when you are comfortably seated. And the perennial dilemma in Llanarmon is whether to stay in the Hand or the West. The Hand offers elegance, chic and superb French cuisine: the West is an angler's pub with low beams, huge fireplaces, a good bar for a gossip and the cosiest dining room imaginable.

It doesn't matter commercially which hotel we choose. Because they are both owned by the same man, Tim Alexander. Though his impish sense of humour has led him to tell guests of one hotel out visiting the other and finding him in both, that they have just left his twin brother.

At the moment we marginally prefer the Hand but that is because he has owned it longer than the West and has had more time to create the ambience he wants, which is not to denigrate the welcome that Mary Widdon, who manages the West in fierce competition with her boss, gave us when we went once for a splendid dinner.

Tim is a remarkable man but will probably never forgive us for saying so. When he joined the hotel trade as a teenager, the group manager asked him the job he was aiming for.

"Yours," said Tim. "In ten years."

"In that case," said the group manager, "you had better go into every department in turn so that when you sit in this seat you will know what you are talking about."

Nine years later Tim was the assistant group manager of a chain of luxury London hotels. Then cancer struck. He came near enough to death's door to use a pass-key but characteristically he fought back to health. The trouble was that in his absence the world of the large hotel had changed. The new philosophy was that the customer must be prevented at all costs from getting in the way of the staff. Put him in his cage, give him a TV and a drink dispenser and a radio alarm and pretend that he isn't there.

When you have been given the pass-key to eternity that Tim had just gratefully handed back, you tend to take

51

rather a laid-back view of life. Tim intended to enjoy himself. Since he could only do that if he was running the sort of hotel he would enjoy himself he handed in his notice and bought the Hand.

Now, with his wife Carol, a former merchant banker, he runs a Hand that is outstretched in permanent welcome. He could get an extra star if he would install TV in bedrooms that are already luxurious. He won't because he believes his customers have come for peace and quiet. Breakfast is from 8.30 to 9.30 unless you happen to want it at quarter to eight or quarter to ten. Morning tea is served by a country girl who is all smiles and tender inquiry; the morning paper waits by your plate in a dining room so chic you would never believe it was once a cowshed. The menu is extensive. But if there's anything you fancy which isn't in the list, they will do their best to get it for you.

A bedtime drink? Anything from vintage brandy to malted milk. But the ultimate luxury? It is the only hotel we have been in for years which offers to clean your shoes overnight.

There is a popular song about the welcome in the Welsh hillsides. As we were finding out on visiting those good neighbours the Tanat and the Ceiriog, there's an even warmer welcome in the valleys.

If you want to leave your mark before you leave the Ceiriog walk up the drover's path in the direction of Cynwyd to the cyclists' hut where you can see the Wayfarer's Stone and sign the book he provided for all who walk in the path of Borrow.

Or, if you prefer seeing your spectacular scenery from a motor car, take the mountain road out of Llanarmon towards the Tanat and the great falls of Llanrhaeadr.

The Vale of Llangollen

THE DEE VALLEY

Take the high road — and very steep it is — out of Glyn Ceiriog through Vivod to the A5, turn left in the direction of Corwen and a short drive will bring you to Glyndyfrdwy and to Carrog where Owain Glyndŵr had his palace and where he was invested Prince of Wales.

His wooden Plas was probably situated on the river meadow at the foot of the hillock, crowned now with fir trees, man-grown or natural it is not known. No trace remains of his home but it is unlikely to have been less magnificent than his manor at Sycharth. It is said that in the field to the east of the mound you can trace the outline of the moat which surrounded the palace. Glyndyfrdwy means literally the Glen of the Divine Water. In the Dark Ages, according to Giraldus Cambrensis, the Welsh drew omens of success and failure in battle from changes in the course of the Dee. In the tenth century the river was called Dubr Duiu, once a Welsh name for God. George Barrow recalled a legend that the Dee has its source in two springs whose waters pass through Lake Bala without mingling with the lake water. They symbolised two individuals, Dwy Fawr and Dwy Fach, who escaped the Great Flood. Ian reckons that anyone who has fished this river on a brisk November day for the grayling which abound there, on a day ticket which is surprisingly cheap, could never doubt the Dee's divinity.

It was at his wooden Plas by the Dee that Glyndŵr assumed the title of Prince of Wales. It was very much a family affair.

Present were Owain's brother, Tudor, who was so like

Owain they could only be distinguished by the wart under Owain's eye. There was Owain's eldest son Gruffydd, his brothers-in-law, Howell Gyffin the Dean of St Asaph and his two nephews, two more friends and a poet called "The Crab", who was described as the "rebellious seer". It was from Glyndyfrdwy that travelling bards were sent out to recruit an army. A motley crew they found. It included eleven local men, nine from Yale across the Dee and six from Edeirnion. Two brothers from Corwen, two more from Bala joined. Eighty-one men came from Denbigh, eleven from Ruthin and one hundred and ten from Dyffryn Clwyd.

They were called the Heroes of Cadfan and they were so proud of fighting for Glyndŵr they changed their coat of arms to three greyhounds dormant, a punning reference to the crest of the House of Lancaster, of which the deposed Richard II was a member. There were priests in the army and at least one Englishman; a knight and nine other land-owning neighbours of Owain.

The raggle-taggle army met at Glyndyfrdwy and preparations began for their first attack. The target was to be Lord Grey's castle town of Ruthin...

We chose to continue our tour of Glyndŵr Country by doubling back on our tracks in the Ceiriog Valley and joining the A5 at Chirk, pausing for a brief inspection of one of the Caravan Club's better sites, the Lady Margaret, the entrance to which is virtually at the gates of Chirk Castle.

This route enabled us to compare the Chirk Aqueduct with an even greater example of Telford's genius, the mighty aqueduct at Pontcysyllte which crosses the Dee Valley on superb, self-confident soaring arches. We approached it on another great Telford man-made miracle, the A5 from Shrewsbury to Holyhead, which was built largely at the urging of Irish MPs who wanted a smooth coaching road between Westminster and their constituencies in pre-partition Ireland. The canal itself and the Horseshoe Falls at Llangollen which feed it, were both designed by Telford.

The Froncysyllte aqueduct spans a thousand feet of the Dee Valley at a height of 127 feet above the river. It was opened on 26 November, 1802, with a procession of six barges, including one that contained the band of the Shropshire Volunteers playing lustily over the thunder of a fifteen-gun salute by the Royal Artillery Company. Remembering the primitive building techniques of the day it is a wonder that in the ten years it took to build it only one life was lost.

On the outskirts of Llangollen is a rare example of what can only be described as a stately cottage. It is Plas Newydd, the home of two ladies who, thanks to Telford's new road, were able to entertain the cream of London cultural society. The Ladies of Llangollen, Lady Eleanor Butler and her lover Sarah Ponsonby, lived at Plas Newydd between 1780 and 1831.

When they moved in Plas Newydd was a plain stone house called Pen-y-maed cottage. It wasn't only the name these aristocratic Irish ladies changed. When Miss Ponsonby, the survivor, died in 1831 it was well on its way to becoming the splendid Gothic Folly it now is. The work of transforming it was cheerfully completed by its next owner General Yorke. The once plain frontage is encrusted with wood carvings, some of great antiquity and quality, for which the two ladies must have haunted every demolition sale for miles. Guests who made a second visit were required to bring a present of carved oak.

One very fine carving is a copy of the Golden Door at the Baptistery in Florence and in the knot garden which is part of the five-acre grounds, now a public park, is the pillar of Chester Market Cross which that city's council has been trying without success to retrieve for many years.

We can both remember a time when the inside of Plas Newydd was a disappointment. That is no longer true thanks to the magnificent obsession of one man, Grahame

Fawcett, Principal Engineer, for Glyndŵr District Council which owns the property. Fawcett was Borough Surveyor of Llangollen until local government re-organisation. In his new job he found himself responsible for, among other things, Plas Newydd. He has transformed it with the help of a remarkable ad hoc committee, which includes a kind of benevolent museum mafia drawn from mansions and monuments housing some of the most distinguished collections in Wales.

Slowly, with their assistance and guidance, he is bringing back to the house objects owned by the Ladies which were dispersed by an auction sale when Miss Ponsonby died.

His great coup came by accident. The Ladies, who habitually dressed in riding costume with top hats, would never allow any of the artists who flocked to visit them to paint their portraits. A teenage girl Mary Parker sketched them surreptitiously while visiting with her mother. When she grew up Miss Parker married into the Leighton family, landowners in Shropshire. Quite recently the present baronet, Sir Michael Leighton, visited Plas Newydd and told Fawcett that Mary Parker's painting was hanging in his home, Lowton Hall, near Shrewsbury. He suggested it ought to be in Plas Newydd. He offered to sell the painting and with the aid of a grant from the Victoria and Albert Museum it was bought and now hangs in the Ladies' home.

Even more precious is the book in the glass case below the picture. That too came from Sir Michael's home. It contains all the letters the Ladies wrote to Mary Parker's mother, who had had them bound in a book, together with exquisite water-colour sketches of local scenes done by Mary. Piece by piece other items the Ladies treasured have been returned to the house. It is Grahame Fawcett's intention to restore Plas Newydd to the way it was during the Ladies' lifetime. When we visited him the Spanish leather wallpaper, said to be a gift to the Ladies from the Duke of Wellington, was being restored and the elaborate security system to guard the relics was being completed. That will enable him to seek the loan of the Ladies' exquisite posset cups at present in store at the V and A.

It was the Ladies' boast that in the fifty years they had lived at Plas Newydd they had not left it for longer than thirty hours.

Dr Johnson's friend, Anne Seward, has left a charming description of the house as it was in their day when it had only four apartments: a kitchen, a dining room, a drawing room and a library.

She wrote: "Candles are seldom admitted into the parlour. The ingenious friends have invented a prismatic lantern which occupies the whole elliptical arch of the Gothic door. The lantern is of cut glass, variously coloured, enclosing two lamps. The light it imparts resembles that of a volcano, sanquine and solemn. It is assisted by two glow worm lamps that in little marble reservoirs stand on the chimney-piece. A large Aeolian harp is fixed on one of the windows and when the weather permits them to be opened, it breathes its deep tones to the gale, swelling and softening as that rises and falls.

"This saloon of the Minervas contains the finest editions, superbly bound of the best authors; over them the portraits in miniature and some in larger ovals of their favoured friends."

Some of the pictures, the lantern and the harp which is played by the wind, can still be seen at Plas Newydd.

Not everyone was impressed by the two eccentrics. Sir Walter Scott, who had described Telford's aqueduct as the greatest work of art on earth, was less flattering about the Ladies who he likened to "a couple of hazy or crazy old sailors". But the romantics of the day feted them. Byron sent them a copy of his long poem "Corsair". Wordsworth went one better and composed an ode in the grounds which he dedicated to them. It ended:

"In ours the vale of friendship let this spot
be named, where faithful to a low roofed cot

on Deva's banks, ye have abode so long,
Sisters in love, a love allowed to climb
Even on this earth, above the reach of time."

The sisters were very upset at their home being described as a "low roofed cot" and thought, with some justice, they could have written better poetry themselves. In truth there was something about North Wales which inspired Wordsworth to write some perfectly appalling verse.

Celia instantly took up their cause when she discovered they shared her obsession with cats. They had several including one called "Tatters" and another who perished in a snow drift.

We found yet another interesting house on the outskirts of Llangollen, Plas Eliseg, which is reached by taking the road that runs at the back of the Bridge End Hotel on the far side of the Trefor Bridge in the town centre, incidentally the second Wonder of Wales in Glyndŵr Country and reputed to be the first stone bridge to be built in Wales. But before going to the house and the curiously named World's End we followed the signs "Panorama" for a stunning view of the Dee Valley. Then, back-tracking, we took the footpath to Dinas Brân, the romantic, ruined hilltop castle which watches over the valley. It was originally the fortress of Eliseg, Prince of Powys, who gave his name to the Eliseg rock formation and is renowned for saving Powys from falling into the hands of the English. The Eliseg Pillar, set up by his great-grandson in the ninth century, still stands, in part anyway, above Valle Crucis Abbey of which more later. Continue on this road and you drive over the spectacular Horse-Shoe Pass. Pause as the Drovers once did at the Britannia Inn, a fine place to enjoy the view.

Dinas Brân, watching over Llangollen, is a romantic ruin with an even more romantic history. The present ruin dates back to the reign of Madog ap Gruffydd Maelor, a Prince of Powys who ruled from 1191 - 1236. It is not

known who pulled it down but it was already a ruin in
Henry VII's reign.

In the fourteenth century a celebrated beauty lived
there. Her name was Myfanwy Vychan and a bard called
Hywel ab Einion Lygliw wrote a lovely ode to her. Alas,
his addresses were spurned and the ode ends:

> "How swift on Alban steed I flew
> Thy dazzling countenance to view
> Though hard the steep ascent to gain,
> Thy smiles were harder to obtain..."

After the arduous climb up to Dinas Brân from the road
we were of the opinion that the lady ought to have been
thoroughly ashamed of herself. We consoled ourselves by
gazing at the view and remembering another poem in the
verse form known as an englyn written about Dinas Brân
by an eleventh century poet Roger Kyffin and translated
by Borrow:

> "Gone, gone are thy gates Dinas Brân on the
> height
> Thy warders are blood crows and ravens, I trow,
> Now no-one will wend from the field of the fight
> To the fortress on high, save the raven and
> crow."

Even unluckier in love than Hywel was a prince who was
born in Dinas Brân, Owain, son of Cadwgan, Prince of
Powys. For the setting of that story we retraced our steps
to the road that leads to Plas Eliseg and World's End,
a wooded valley at the foot of the limestone Eliseg Rocks.
The road continues over a ford in a splendid, if
hair-raising, drive up a single track route over the
mountains to Minera and Mold. Ian refuses to go further
than Plas Eliseg. It is just possible the reason is, as he
claims, that he can never tear himself away from the house
because it is so intriguing. Such a perfect example of an

Elizabethan manor house in such an inaccessible spot is incongruous; its history is even more fascinating than its architecture. It was to a house on this site that Owain brought his kidnapped "bride".

The story began at Christmas in 1108 when Cadwgan held a great eisteddfod at his court in Cardigan. Among the guests was a beautiful girl called Nest, the daughter of Rhys, Prince of Deheubarth. As a child hostage in the English court she had been almost immediately seduced by Henry I who then married her off to Gerald of Windsor.

Owain saw this luckless lady at his father's feast, fell in love with her and impetuously carried both her and her two children off to his highly defensible lair at World's End. His father ordered him to return Nest to her husband but Owain would only agree, and that grudgingly, to return her two children.

As an earlier traveller, the Rev. S. Baring Gould put it with delightful understatement: "This outrage was the occasion of civil war."

History was not done with Plas Eliseg however. The tenant in the seventeenth century was Colonel John Jones, Oliver Cromwell's brother-in-law. Jones was a farmer's son who married Cromwell's sister Catherine. In the Civil War he laid unsuccessful siege to Harlech Castle. He had a chequered career. He was one of the regicides who signed Charles I's death warrant and was rewarded by Cromwell with the Governorship in Dublin, only to die, hanged, drawn and quartered, at the Restoration for his part in the king's death. Samuel Pepys passed his smoking remains.

High above the house where Cromwell's regicide brother-in-law dwelt lives a rather more urbane judge. Mr Justice Knox Mawer was a judge in the South Seas. He and his wife June, a former presenter of Woman's Hour and well-known broadcaster, inhabit three cottages hugging the mountainside under the Eliseg rocks. Mr Justice Knox Mawer is one of the wittiest judges in history. Among the causes he tried was one when he put a tribe of whirling dervishes on probation for a breach of the peace. Once he obeyed to the letter the instructions of the Colonial Office to conform to local practice by sharing his judicial responsibility with a Shark God. Fortunately he never had the embarrassing situation which his predecessor as judge in the Cannibal Islands experienced. The jury ate the defendant! June, his wife and an old and dear friend, spends half the year in the workmen's cottages they have knocked together with her actress daughter Vanessa.

Halfway between the Horseshoe Pass and the town of Llangollen is a fifteenth century church, restored with all the regrettable enthusiasm of the nineteenth century but nevertheless owning some interesting pieces of fifteenth century glass. The poet Browning visited the church and was charmed by it.

Restoration is less evident in the parish church of St Collen, a former Roman soldier who slew a pagan giant and from whom the town takes its mutated name. The sixteenth century wooden ceilings over the nave are interesting, particularly the section with delightful gold angels on the hammer beam. They are claimed to have come from Valle Crucis Abbey. The Ladies of Llangollen and their faithful servant, Mary Carryll, who helped them when they eloped together from Ireland, are buried there.

St Collen, whom the church celebrates, is chiefly famous for vanquishing Gwyn ap Nudd, the King of the Welsh Fairies, the Tylwyth Teg. Gwyn ap Nudd summoned St Collen to his kingdom where he asked him, "Did you ever see men better dressed than my servants here, in red and blue?"

St Collen answered him, "The red on one side denotes burning and the blue freezing" and so saying he sprinkled the fairy host with holy water and they instantly disappeared.

The hospitality was rather better at Valle Crucis Abbey whose magnificent ruin so impressed John Ruskin, who incidentally thought the Dee Valley was the loveliest in the world, that he intended to call a book he proposed on British Abbeys "Valle Crucis". It was the first Gothic abbey to be built in Britain in 1200 A.D. by Prince Madog of Dinas Brân.

Owain Glyndŵr's bard Iolo Goch, who was a landowner in the valley, is reputed to be buried here although Robert of Lancaster, the abbot, did not approve of the rebellion. Early one morning he met Glyndŵr walking in the hills. "Sir Abbot, you have risen too early," Glyndŵr said. "No, my son," replied the abbot drily, "tis you who have risen too early, by a hundred years." It was an unwise remark. Glyndŵr later razed the bishop's palace.

The abbots of Valle Crucis have been a colourful lot. The first abbot Philip was in trouble for rarely celebrating mass, his successor Dafydd ab Ieuan was the illegitimate son of a monk and his successor, in 1528, was a burglar and a highwayman. He was arrested for forging coins, escaped from Banbury Gaol, was recaptured at Valle Crucis and died in the Tower of London.

Whatever their personality defects the abbots of Valle Crucis were splendid hosts. Although Cistercians were taught by St Benedict to shun luxury at Valle Crucis they became very wealthy sheep farmers. Officially they lived a stricter life than other monks; in fact they believed in living well. They had their own bard, Guto'r Glyn, but they were surely less than pleased when he gave the game away in a poem in which he described a feast at the abbey:

> "There shall we have tables loaded with gifts,
> Much drinking and various victuals,
> In the Place of Egwestl — several dishes.
> There is an old liquor to make us merry,
> Pale and dark metheglin.
> We shall have bragget and sharp ale from the
> pipes, wine and nuts;
> We shall have a thousand apples for dessert,
> And grace, honour and dignity.
> Honey, grapes, the fruit of orchards
> And of the fortress of Yale, and carols
> And fire which shall make the old feel younger

There during dinner will arise the strains of
organs
Vocal and instrumental music."

None of us who love the town and its environs are
surprised that Llangollen was the destination of the
world's first charbanc trip in 1906. The charabanc was
chartered by 18 members of the Liverpool Bowling Club.

We have a special tenderness for Llangollen because it
was there we met for the first time when we were sent by
our respective newspapers to report on the International
Eisteddfod. Ian claims to have been going there so long he
can remember it when it was a duet. Be that as it may, it
has become, surely, the biggest singing festival on earth.
Yet it started so humbly. Just before the end of the war in
1945 newspaperman Harold Tudor was walking in the hills
near the town when he heard a milk-boy singing a hymn as
he pedalled his bike down a lane.

In his book "Making the Nations Sing" Tudor recalls,
"In this ancient Welsh lane was a strange, ennobling
contrast — a boy untouched by the turmoil encompassing
his leaders' world, a boy with a confident heart and a
message on his lips."

That gave Tudor, by this time an official with the British
Council, the idea of an international singing festival but it
took time to translate the idea into action. Starting with a
£500 overdraft and a borrowed marquee was a gamble, but
not so great a gamble as sending out invitations to
countries like Germany and Italy, our recent enemies. But
it worked. Indeed it worked so magnificently that when in
1986 the Eisteddfod celebrated its first forty years it
attracted choirs and folk groups from fifty different
countries. In Eisteddfod time Llangollen turns itself
overnight into a kind of Welsh Hollywood musical. The
Eisteddfod ground is a natural amphitheatre; the Cultural
Centre, the new Information Centre and the whole town
are thronged with singers and dancers in every conceivable
national costume. By tradition drink is not sold on the field
but in Wales there is always a way round. In Llangollen a

gate in the fence hard by the pavilion leads to the Jenny Jones, the informal meeting place for contestants. Nothing could be more suitable. The original Jenny was a local milk-maid so beautiful that she became the subject of a Victorian ballad.

There is a great deal to do in Llangollen. There is a motor museum which brings tears to the eyes of advanced (in years, not ability) motorists. It is at Pentre Felin and to all intents and purposes it is like stepping back in time to a garage in the thirties. There is nostalgia too at the railway station where former LMS steam engines ply two miles of track that will eventually run as far as Corwen. In happier times the service ran from Ruabon to Dolgellau and was universally agreed to be among the loveliest rail journeys in Britain. Like so much of Britain's rural railway it was vandalised in 1963 by Doctor Beeching but saved from total extinction by enthusiasts who formed the Llangollen Railway Society.

Happily there was no Beeching to ruin the continuous tradition of the Shropshire Union Canal which Thomas Telford worked on as a young engineer. It has been open since 1884. The Boat Centre on the wharf opened on the same day and has been carrying passengers ever since. Our fancy was for a short trip in a horse-drawn barge and a prowl round the Canal Museum when we returned. It has working models which are quite fascinating and explains far better than words just what a gruelling business not only digging a canal was but barging too.

Also in Llangollen, most appropriately, is the European Centre for traditional and regional cultures which regularly hosts exhibitions. A recent one on Old Money recalled the days when small merchant banks all over Wales used their own banknotes before a more centralised system took over.

The river Dee runs through the centre of the town, spanned by the first stone bridge to be built in Wales. It takes its name from the artful Bishop Trefor who rebuilt it in 1346. He was first in the service of Richard II, abandoned him when his ruin was likely and joined his enemy Owain Glyndŵr. He advised Owain and arranged a treaty between Wales and France but when Owain began to lose, he abandoned him too and joined the service of Henry IV.

On the far side of the bridge, next to an admirable restaurant, are the steps which lead to Victoria Promenade, a riverside park of enormous charm.

In 1987 the town's musical reputation widened even further when the first Internation Jazz Festival in Wales was held there.

* * *

Corwen keeps its secrets. It is on the road to everywhere. The A5 splits in half a town which would otherwise have been a sheer delight to amble round. It has some notable ancient pubs, the Harp, the Royal Oak and the Crown, where we had the finest plate of country-cured ham and eggs it has been our good fortune to taste. The Crown is an enchanting pub, cosily panelled and warmly welcoming and the bustle and roar of the traffic outside its door is muffled and unobtrusive. Not the least of its joys for us — apart from the landlord Warwick Sims and his wife Valerie — was a regular customer, Dai Bugler, an old warrior who fought in every campaign in the last war and before, from the North-West Frontier through Dunkirk to the Second Front. When we met he was living a quiet life as a grave-digger and gardener at the hidden gem of Corwen, the parish church of St Mael and St Sulien.

The church is a delightful surprise. Walk through a lychgate set in a wall and the twentieth century disappears from your mind. The church is set at the end of a path which crosses springy green turf and is lined with penitent stones, which are gravestones with hollows in which penitents kneel to pray — presumably for chromium-plated knees. Over the door is a lintel carved with a very early crucifix, which gullible tourists were once told was an imprint Owain Glyndŵr made when he threw his sword at the church. The churchyard contains an interesting memento of the time when Corwen was an important railway town. It is the gravestone of Owen Owen, an engine driver who died at the age of 29. It reads:

> "His life is over,
> Death has put on the brake,
> His soul has been signalled
> Its long journey to make.
> When death sounds his whistle
> The steam of life fails
> And his mortal clay shunted
> Till the Last Judgment calls."

In the north porch of the church is a monolith round which the wall has been built. This is "The pointed stone in the frozen rock" and an interesting legend is attached. This site was not the first choice of the thirteenth century congregation. They planned to build their place of worship in another part of the graveyard. But whatever they built by day was mysteriously moved by night to the place where the church now stands. They built well and for once restoration was sympathetic. There is a fine font, twelfth century or earlier, and in former times the water it held was always brought from St Sulien's well, a good two miles away across the Dee. Notice, inside, the memorial to one of Nelson's sailors who seems to have fought in every sea battle for the better part of a century.

Beside the church is the only public memorial to the town's greatest hero that I have been able to find. It is the Owain Glyndŵr Hotel where Borrow slaked his not inconsiderable thirst. Its other and greater claim to fame was that the first public eisteddfod was held there in the eighteenth century.

The most handsome building in this likeable town is the old workhouse. When it was built in 1840 it had an Inspector of Nuisances and tramps were given a bed across the road only after they had smashed rock into a hundredweight of chippings. Since it was no longer needed for the purpose for which it was built the workhouse has served many different masters. Now it is the home of a community, every one of the 35 members of which has been cured of seemingly incurable diseases. The Orissor Trust calls itself a college of common sense. It is completely self-supporting, its members follow a strictly vegetarian diet and include one very famous man. In the early 1980's Frank Serpico, the New York detective who all but got himself killed exposing corruption in the N.Y. Police Department, arrived at the community broken in body and mind. He stayed a year in Corwen before returning to the U.S. a new man.

It was in the hills above Corwen that Owain Gwynedd mustered his men before the battle with Henry I in the Ceiriog. It is said that the men mustered at Caer Drewyn, an ancient hill fort.

Further along the road to Ruthin is the village of Bryneglwys, for many Americans a place of pilgrimage. The man who gave his name to Yale University came from an ancient family whose home was here. Elihu Yale is buried in Wrexham churchyard under the inscription which reads:

> "Born in America, in Europe bred,
> In Africa travelled, in Asia wed,
> Where long he lived and thrived, in London dead.
> Much good, some ill he did, so hope all's even
> And that his soul through mercy's gone to heaven."

It is curious that Elihu, the son of a Pilgrim Father who left the ancestral home Plas-yn-Iâl to settle in the New World, should have chosen to be buried at Wrexham. In the parish church at Bryneglwys there is a Yale chapel.

This part of the northern slopes of the Dee Valley has

less pleasant associations for Welshmen with a strong sense of history. For it was at nearby Rug, now the home of Lord Newborough, that Gruffydd ap Cynan, King of North Wales, was ambushed and carried off by Hugh the Fat, the Norman earl of Chester. He kept him in chains at his fortress in Chester and was in the habit of exhibiting him chained in Chester market. A young man from Yale visiting the market was so incensed to see his prince spat upon and humbled that he rode into the market, gathered up the prince, chains and all, and galloped off to freedom.

There is everywhere in Glyndŵr Country a sense of ancient place and links with far-off inhabitants are always being found. In July 1987 a local historian John Dutton discovered in the Bryneglwys Valley a Roman military road which stretched from Chester to Corwen and was used by members of the Twentieth Legion in their occupation of Wales. The road dates from around 73 A.D. and excavations have shown it to have kerbs and side drains. Mr Dutton has tracked twenty miles of the road and spent two years searching for the Bryneglwys section. On hillside terraces the road narrows to 3.04 metres and there are signs of river fords, roadside quarries and signal posts. From Corwen the road fords the River Dee close to Green Lane bridge where, curving to the north-east, it passes Moel Fodif and runs along the valley floor at the side of the A5104, where there is also an ancient drovers' road.

The A5 runs through Glyndŵr Country like an asphalt artery, but we left it briefly beyond Corwen to go off the Beaten Track.

The Edeyrnion Valley is easily missed by the casual tourist rushing either to the Welsh Coast or the English border. A pity. It is delightful. There are two villages, Cynwyd and Llandrillo, both on the banks of the Dee. At Llandrillo the Tyddyn Llan Hotel is at its busiest in the winter when it takes shooting parties from all over Britain. Even the owner is a refugee from "shooting." He is former TV Director Peter Kindred who with his wife Briget also

70

restored a charming period house. All Saints Church, Llangan, dates from 12 th Cent, disused now, it contains ancient wall paintings, recently discovered and restored by Cadw as is the Chapel on Lord Newborough's Estate at Rhug. Both open to public in 1988.

As we let the A5 take us out of Corwen to our next destination, Denbigh, we reflected on the sheer sophistication of its design, the elegance of its engineering and its durability. We put new words to the old song, "Motorways may crumble and bridges may tumble, They're only meant for a day. The A5 is here to stay…"

The A5 is the most sympathetic of roads. It makes no brutal challenge to the landscape; though it runs through some of the toughest terrain in Britain, there is comfort in travelling it. When it was first built as a coach road of 107 miles from Shrewsbury to Holyhead, nowhere did the horses have to slow down to a walk. Even through Snowdonia, at its highest over the mountains and along the Nant Ffrancon pass, the gradient never exceeds one in twenty-two. It is durable. Telford built as the Romans did. First he levelled and drained, next he laid down a solid pavement of large stones, broad end down, closely set and levelled; finally he added a layer of stones no bigger than walnuts.

Denbigh Castle

Photo: Wales Tourist Board

DENBIGH, BRENIG AND THE VALE OF CLWYD

Until the A5 was built Glyndŵr Country was all but inaccessible to tourists. Even today, turn off it at Cerrigydrudion for Denbigh, and you go fifty years back in time to the easy days of pre-war motoring, bowling along empty roads, passing picnic places every yard of the way, to one of the least used tourist paradises in Britain.

Brenig Lake is man-made. We didn't believe it when we first saw it but it is true. Man planted the forest which surrounds it, flooded the valley and now fishes and sails on its surface. In 1976 it was opened by the Prince of Wales and is part now of a 2,439-acre playground. The statistics are mind-boggling. The lake is two and a half miles long and holds 13,500 million gallons of water covering 919 acres. The choice of activities is just as impressive. Sailing, canoeing, board-sailing, sub-aqua diving, game fishing, picnicking, nature trailing, archaeological trailing, even, in winter, ski-trailing. There is bird watching, a Visitor Centre with an interpretive exhibition, a cafe, shopping in the craft centre. Similar attractions are also available in the Clocaenog Forest nearby.

With all the pleasures it offers it is easy to forget that Brenig is a Welsh Water Authority undertaking with a serious purpose. It is a regulating reservoir. From the lake water flows into the River Brenig to top up the river Dee when water levels fall there. The supply from Celyn reservoir and Lake Bala and from Brenig is co-ordinated by computer, boosting low summer supplies and preventing winter flooding. Eventually the water at Brenig will flow out of taps in Liverpool, Chester and Deeside.

It is a fitting monument to the ingenuity of man who first came to these parts 7,000 years ago in the Stone Age. Around 4,000 years ago, in the Bronze Age, he dug one of the largest burial grounds, the Ring Cairn, that has ever been excavated. In 1987 archaeologists found the remains of a Hafod — a Welsh upland farm — where shepherds brought their flocks during the summer months. Since the first burial grounds were discovered during the excavation work to form Lake Brenig experts have been looking for traces of the homes of the people who dug them. The circular stone Hafod which they found at Bryn Helen, a remote hamlet at Pentrellyncymer, is the oldest dwelling in Clwyd. It is covered now but there is still plenty of evidence in the area of early man. Round the shores of the lake a gentle ramble will take you past eleven archaeological sites.

We found Brenig and Mynydd Hiraethog, the high moorland between Pentrefoelas and Bylchau, wonderful walking country and were not surprised that among the farm-workers who lived here in the nineteenth century there were thirteen poets. They worked land that had been awarded to the Abbey of Aberconwy in 1198 by Llywelyn ab Iorwerth and is still called "tir abad uchaf", the high land of the abbot.

We were intrigued by a later monument, a gaunt Gothic ruin that seemed to brood over us on the skyline whichever way we turned. We remembered that when Granada TV were filming their Sherlock Holmes series, the waterfall Pistyll Rhaeadr, at Llanrhaeadr-ym-Mochnant, was used for the Reichenbach Falls, the scene of the death struggle between Holmes and Moriarty. This ruin on the moors above Brenig seemed pure Conan Doyle. We found on inquiry that it has appeared in many TV films including Wuthering Heights. It was a shooting lodge built in 1913 by an immensely wealthy Merseyside tycoon, Lord Davenport. It is called Gwylfa Hiraethog and until the first world war grouse shooting parties stayed there in tremendous luxury. When war broke out it was abandoned.

Today we get along rather better with the wildlife and birdwatchers can enjoy rare treats. On the highest moorland at Marial Gwyn there are buzzards and ravens, occasional osprey visit the lake. We picnicked by an old stone bridge, Pont y Brenig, before wandering along a mile and a quarter of nature trail and think we saw both black and red grouse.

So spectacular is Brenig that its neighbour the Alwen Reservoir is sometimes missed by the visitor, though few ever miss the Sportsman's Arms, near Brenig, which has the distinction of being the highest inn in Wales.

Although it doesn't make the claim itself, we think that The Filling Station qualifies as the highest garage in Wales. When we came across it on the moors on the Pentrefoelas road between Denbigh and Brenig we were delighted. We were running dangerously low on petrol and after the Filling Station the next petrol station is a good 15 miles away in Betws-y-Coed. We were even more delighted when we discovered it was a kind of holiday home for Land-Rovers. No-one ever has undecided views about the Land-Rover, which incidentally was invented on Anglesey in North Wales. People either love them or hate them. We love them. We've worn one out and are on our second, which should outlast us. Pauline and Mike Morris are Land-Rover fanatics too. They are members of the Land-Rover Club and don't like really repairing any other kind of vehicle, though of course, they will.

One fact above all others endeared Denbigh to Ian. It was warmly recommended by his hero Dr Sam Johnson, the famous eighteenth century dictionary maker and scholar, who stayed here in 1774 on his tour of Wales. Indeed, Denbigh was one of the few things about Wales that Johnson liked. He spoke highly of the town, where he was entertained at Gwaenynog, a delightful mansion about a mile and a half from Denbigh Castle. He writes warmly of the welcome he was given by the Myddelton of the day. During his stay the Doctor is said to have designed the drawing room and music room, which were added to the ancient house at that time. He used to walk by the banks of the river Ystrad to declaim poetry in a quiet spot. Mr Myddelton thought to please him by erecting the stone temple on the river bank which contains a Grecian urn. Dr Johnson, who had a morbid fear of death, was furious. "It looks like an intention to bury me alive," he thundered. "I would as well see my friend, however benevolent and hospitable, quietly inured..." Nevertheless it is a lovely spot and we enjoyed the riverside walk to reach it.

Denbigh has many claims to literary fame. H.M. Stanley, the foreign correspondent who found Dr Livingstone in the African jungle, was born in the town but there is a "memorial" at Gwaenynog that will be nearer to young hearts.

In Victorian times Beatrix Potter was a frequent visitor to the house. She came to see her uncle Fred Burton. His grandson, Captain Oliver Burton, lives at Gwaenynog today and recalls his grandfather as a large man with a bushy beard. He thinks he was probably the model for Mr McGregor, the gardener in the Tale of the Flopsy Bunnies. Certainly much of the furniture, the house and the gardens are illustrated there.

When we visited, Captain Burton's grand-daughter Frances, a 19-year-old horticulturalist, was restoring the gardens to the way they looked in the illustrations. She was hoping to get them in shape in time to join the National Gardens Scheme in 1988. Visitors are welcome but should telephone first.

The visit should especially interest children. Beside the joy of seeing the pictures of the Flopsie Bunnies come to life and exploring the potting shed with its mementoes of their favourite book they can watch ice-cream being made. Faced with the prospect of having to destroy part of their 180 herd of cows to meet milk quotas, Frances' parents, Major and Mrs Tom Smith, turned the old dairy into an ice-cream factory. Now their Denbigh Farmhouse Ices, made to a secret family recipe, are being licked by Peter Rabbit lovers everywhere.

One irony. Remember the letter which ran:

"To Mr McGregor, Gardener's Cottage.

"Dear Sir,

I write to ask whether your spring cabbages are ready?

Yours truly, Peter Rabbit."

Nowadays, to Captain Burton's chagrin, the estate is so over-run by rabbits that not only his cabbages but his young trees are disappearing.

The Captain's great uncle bought the estate from yet another branch of the Myddelton family who had lived there since medieval times, though not always on the side of the law. He showed us a picture of William Myddelton drawn in 1741. Though he was High Sheriff of the county at the time the cartoon shows him in Newgate Prison where he was sent for fiddling an election result.

His disgrace did not rob him of his place among his ancestors and descendants in St Marcellus, the parish church. The church is well worth a visit for the memorials alone. Among them is one to the great antiquarian and one of the first Welsh map-makers, Humphrey Llwyd, who prophesied his own death at 41 a year before it happened. But to most Welshmen the church is thought of only as the burial ground of Twm o'r Nant, Tom of the Dingle, the Welsh Shakespeare, or, as he was baptised, Thomas Edwards. He was born in 1739, the son of a poor peasant family, but he will be immortal in Welsh literature as a satirist and playwright. His family were so poor that he only had three weeks' schooling before he was sent out to earn his living in the fields. In his autobiography he wrote:

"As soon as I had learned to spell and write a few words I conceived a mighty desire to learn to write; so I went in quest of elderberries to make me ink and my first essay in writing was trying to copy on the sides of leaves of a book the letters of the words I read. It happened however that a shop in the village caught fire and the greater part of it was burnt, only a few trifles being saved, and among the scorched articles my mother got for a penny were a number of sheets of paper burned at the edges and sewed them together to make copy books for me."

Tom was determined. He borrowed books from a chapel reader; he learned from a local poet for whom he worked as a copyist. In those days young boys made up morality plays called "interludes". The first that Tom wrote was stolen by a youth from Anglesey. His second was bought by a troupe of touring actors who rewarded him with a pot of ale. He was on his way to success until he was attacked by the brother of a girl he had mocked. Hearing that he had killed the man, Tom took to the hills above Pentrefoelas. The man, however, was not dead and Tom was able to return and marry. He was 24 when he settled down as a wood-cutter near Denbigh but he spent so much of his time helping others that he got into debt. He wrote to pay off his debts and made enough to set up as a carrier. He had made a fortune when he fell for the second time.

He made himself responsible for a bill for his uncle. When it wasn't paid he was sued and had to flee to South Wales. He kept a turnpike but even then he was unlucky. He was swindled by his employer.

Broke once again, Tom turned to writing and once again his work was an enormous success. He returned to Denbigh, set up as a stone-mason and died at 71, mourned by everyone who knew him. His writing has great elegance and wit and, who knows, had he had a more settled private life we might be talking about Shakespeare now as "the English Twm o'r Nant".

It was to Denbigh Castle that the news of the greatest Welsh victory of the Glyndŵr War was brought. A party of forty men, headed by the Tudor brothers from Anglesey, crept into Conwy Castle on Easter Eve while the garrison was at church. While some of the Tudor warriors manned the castle, others lay in ambush and when the garrison marched down the street of the strategically crucial town they charged and in the fight that followed the town was gutted.

Denbigh Castle was the seat of the Chief Justice of North Wales and at that time he was one of the most charismatic warriors in Europe, "Harry Hotspur". As we stood by the massive Burgess Gate, which was once part of the impregnable town walls, we tried to imagine what followed when he heard the news of the fall of Conwy. At the head of a mounted column of 120 men and 130 archers Hotspur — he was given the name when he was still a boy by the Scots against whom he was fighting — galloped off to Conwy.

He laid siege to the castle for over a month. Then Hotspur struck a dreadful deal with the Tudors. They handed over nine of their men as scapegoats to be hung, drawn and quartered and were in return allowed to leave the castle unharmed.

When Hotspur commanded its garrison Denbigh Castle was already old. It stands on the site of a palace of Llywelyn the Great but there was probably a fort here in pre-historic times.

The present castle was begun in October 1282 by Edward I after he had wrested the earlier fort from Llywelyn's brother Dafydd ap Gruffydd whose principal stronghold it was. Edward handed it over to a henchman, Henry de Lacy, whom the king created Lord of the Manor. It was not a lucky appointment. Within twelve years the Welsh had recaptured it and when, once again, he was in control de Lacy's son fell down the Goblin Tower and was killed.

Although Glyndŵr attacked the castle and burned the town it became an integral part of his kingdom. In 1402 he had captured Hotspur's son-in-law, Edmund Mortimer, uncle of the infant Earl of March and Lord of Denbigh Castle. Captivity proved so attractive to Mortimer that he married Owain's daughter.

In 1563 Elizabeth I sold the castle to her favourite Robert Dudley, Earl of Leicester. He did little to the castle but began to build what was planned to replace St Asaph and become the biggest Protestant cathedral in Wales. Unfortunately he ran out of money and we can see it today below the castle hill and beyond the tower which is all that remains of Denbigh's first religious building, St Hilary's Within the Walls. A cathedral is a curious memorial to the grasping Earl who squeezed every penny he could from his luckless vassals. When two landowners protested he had them hanged.

As we stood under the dramatic arch of the Great Gatehouse, one of the most magnificent survivals of medieval castle architecture, prowled round the walls and looked down on the Earl of Leicester's ill-fated cathedral a sudden thought struck us. The ruins would make a perfect setting for an arts festival. Orchestral concerts, even operas, in the cathedral and the whole of Shakespeare's "King Plays" performed in the castle.

The vision carried us happily through lunch in the pretty panelled dining room of the Bull Hotel, one of the oldest and most interesting of the many hostelries in the town. We reflected on the old Welsh tale of how Denbigh got its name.

Sir John Salusbury, a medieval knight who was said to have two thumbs on each hand, was petitioned by the townspeople to rid them of a winged serpent which had its lair in a cave in the castle rock. After a mighty battle Sir John killed the serpent and carried its head back to the town. When the people saw him a great shout went up, "Dim Dych", they cried, which means "No more dragon". If you say it quickly it does sound like Denbigh (especially in Welsh) and it is more romantic than the other tradition which says that Denbigh is a corruption of Dinas Bach, Little Fortress.

A very active family the Salusburys, who, by the way, were to inherit Glyndŵr's estates in the Dee Valley. Dr Johnson's friend, the indefatigable blue-stocking Esther Thrale, was a Salusbury, as also was the Elizabethan Catherine de Berain — the mother of the historic rather than the fabulous Sir John — who rejoices in the hard-earned title "Mother of Wales" because so many families descend from her. She was brought to the funeral of her first husband, a Salusbury, by landowner Maurice Wynn, who took the opportunity to propose. She had to refuse. On the way to the church she had agreed to marry Sir Richard Clough. But she said that when Sir Richard died she would be happy to marry Wynn and indeed did. Her fourth husband Edward Thelwell survived her.

Sir John, whose tomb and effigy can be seen in St Marcella's, was a doughty fighter. His estates were called Lleweni, literally the Lion's Den, after he had killed a white lioness with a blow of his naked fist. He otherthrew, in a wrestling match, a giant whose walking stick was a cart axle tree with a crowbar driven through it. Sir John, it was said, could pull up a forest of trees with his bare hands.

It was a Salusbury who commanded the garrison at Denbigh during the Civil War when it protected Charles I, and he was, perhaps, the finest Salusbury of them all.

Sir William Salusbury was known to his men as Old Blue Stockings because of his fancy hose but he was a warrior rather than a dandy. He held the castle until it was the last unconquered Cavalier stronghold in Britain. The Roundhead troops were commanded by an old friend and neighbour Thomas Myddelton who begged Salusbury to surrender. But Blue Stockings held out from the summer of 1646 until the king commanded him to give up the castle in November. Even in defeat he was defiant. He watched from the top of the Goblin Tower as his men marched out, still bearing arms as a tribute to their courage. Then he flung the castle keys down on the heads of the Roundheads and shouted, "The world is yours, make it your dunghill."

Denbigh has yet another claim to artistic fame. The

eighteenth century actress Mrs Jordan, who wrote "The Bluebells of Scotland", was born at Nantglyn Plas, five miles from the town. Charles Lamb wrote of her and of the way her voice "with her steady melting eye" sank into his heart when she played Viola in Twelfth Night. She retired to France where she died at the age of 50 in 1816.

Above all else the Vale of Clwyd is a motorist's paradise of easy driving on almost empty roads. It is a grand place for outings and pleasant excursions exploring the glorious verdant countryside. The Vale is achingly lovely and the time we spent pottering round the ancient churches on a glorious, sunny October day is one of our happiest memories.

Vale churches are venerable and kindly. They have more often than not twin aisles and it is said that the reason is that one was used to shelter pilgrims.

The first we visited was Llangwyfan (the key is held by Mrs Bandy at the Whitehouse bungalow on the Llandyrnog road). The village stocks outside the gate strike the only hostile note. The low-slung stone church, no bigger than a barn, is homely. From its churchyard the Vale stretched before us from the rocks of Eyarth right down to the sea. So stunned were we by the view that we almost missed the tombstone of Foulke Jones who was born in 1691 and died in 1807, thus living in three centuries, which should surely qualify him for the Guinness Book of Records. The church contains a splendid font on which there are carvings depicting the Great Flood, which argues a sense of humour in the mason. The bell, which has summoned centuries of parishioners to worship, is built into a wooden pulley wheel.

The Vale of Clwyd is justly called the Garden of Wales and it seemed that wherever we went the loveliness around us was accompanied by the sound of water. The Clwyd is by no means a mighty river but it seems ubiquitous and its song is nowhere more charming than its tributors at St Dyfnog's glorious church at Llanrhaeadr. We couldn't find the tombstone which, according to a Victorian book on our shelves, is to be found there. Pity, it has a great ring to it.

> "Here lyeth the body of
> on a Welch Gentleman.
> Here lyeth the body of
> John Ap Robert, Ap Porth, Ap
> David, Ap Griffith, Ap David
> Vaughan, Ap Blethyn, Ap
> Griffith, ap Meredith,
> Ap Jerworth, Ap Heilin, Ap
> Cowryd, Ap Cadvan, Ap
> Alawgwa, Ap Cadell, The
> King of Powys, Who
> Departed This Life, The
> xx Day of March, In The
> Year of Our Lord God
> 1642, And Of
> His Age xcv."

St Dyfnog was a deeply austere man who established a hermitage on this site in the sixth century. As a penance he would stand under the fall of water in what became his well, though it was probable, as with many early Christian settlements, that he chose a pagan "holy" well on which to graft a Christian tradition. Be that as it may, the well acquired a tremendous reputation as a cure-all. Writing in the seventeenth century, the Denbigh antiquarian Humphrey Lloyd told how it was "a bath much frequented; the water heals scabs, itches etc. Some say t'would cure ye pox."

It was said that the donations of pilgrims enabled the church, in 1533, to buy the magnificent Jesse window for which St Dyfnog's is famous. Another tradition has it that at the time of the dissolution of the monasteries it was brought secretly from Basingwerk Abbey to prevent Henry VIII, the mad son of the first Tudor king, Henry VII, from destroying it. It was certainly hidden during the Civil War. The church still has the massive chest into which it was placed and then buried in the woods at the back of the church. It is widely acknowledged to be the finest piece of medieval glass in Britain but, alas, it had been taken out for a third time when we visited. The church needs £160,000 to combat subsidence which has caused the walls to buckle. Only a chronic shortage of funds prevented us from writing out a cheque on the spot but Celia knows where her first bounty goes if she ever has a pools win.

In its absence there were still many things of interest to note and admire, among them the meticulous coats of arms on the nineteenth century tomb of a member of the powerful Mostyn family. The tomb also bears a touching tribute to the man from his wife who wanted to be buried "as near to him as possible". The church porch itself is exquisitely carved and was probably once part of a rood screen.

It is likely there was a companion window to the Jesse. This is now plain glass and perhaps replaces an original smashed by the Roundhead troops — largely made up of Londoners and commanded by General Mytton himself — who sacked the church. We almost overlooked a fine piece of fifteenth century glass, possibly part of the window which was smashed. It was found in the nineteenth century under a heap of rubbish in a cottage, no doubt hidden from the Roundheads by a pious parishioner.

The Jesse window, apart, the great glory of St Dyfnog's is its carved roof. Over the sactuary it is barrelled, intricately carved with vine leaves and supported by angels holding the instruments of the passion.

A nice ecumenical touch to be noted in the graveyard is the last resting place of Ann Parry, who, in the eighteenth century, brought Methodism to the district. As she lay dying she wished that her body would remain as incorruptible as her soul. Forty-two years later her grave was opened and her body was in perfect condition. Six years after that when the grave was opened for a second time she was seen still to be perfectly preserved. We hope that from now on she will be allowed to wait in peace for Judgment Day.

St Gynhafal has only one church dedicated to him. It is but a little way from our last port of call but worth the detour. It is fifteenth century and has some fine examples of seventeenth century carving. The sense of continuity which is so much part of the fabric of Glyndŵr Country is manifest in the communion cup which has been in continual use since 1616.

We confess, though, that our original reason for visiting Llangynhafal on our way to Ruthin was literary.

Plas-yn-llan, the half-timbered house next to the church, was the home of Robert Jones, Wordsworth's great friend and companion on the ramble through France, Switzerland and Italy in 1790, where he wrote his first major poetry. Wordsworth described himself and Jones in a letter to his sister: "Our manner of carrying our bundles, which is upon our heads; with each an oak stick in their hands, contributes not a little to the general curiosity which we seem to excite."

The oak sticks were useful. Although he was studying to be a parson, Jones, according to de Quincey, used them for "administering punishment to restive and mutinous landlords who presented huge reckonings with one hand and with the other a huge cudgel..."

Wordsworth twice stayed with Jones at Plas-yn-llan. He remarked on "the sunsets which give such splendour to the Vale of Clwyd."

Exactly in the centre of the Vale of Clwyd is Llanynys, the church among the water meadows, formerly known as Llanfor, the Great Church. A yew tree in the Glebe Field marks the exact centre of the Vale and the main road from Denbigh to Ruthin cuts the parish in half. All of which caused us to wonder why Llanynys is so hard to find. We missed it one day, gave up looking for it on another and almost went home without seeing it on the third. That would have been a tragedy because this hidden-away church is the custodian of a great treasure. It is a huge medieval wall painting of St Christopher, which was hidden for centuries under layers of whitewash until it was discovered in 1967 by the vicar, the Rev. L. Parry Jones. It was painted in the first half of the fifteenth century and might even date to the Glyndŵr War. It is the work of a master and the halo round the head of the Christ Child on the St Christopher's shoulder was originally gold leaf. Paintings of the patron saint of travellers are characteristically found near to the church door. It is said that he protects against storms and lighting and that whoever looked on him would neither faint nor fall that day.

It seemed a fitting way to leave the lovely Vale. There is much more to be said about the church but there is no need to set it down here. The Rev. Parry Jones has produced what we are agreed is the most delightul and informative booklet we have found in a church. We hope all our readers will buy one and help to keep this lovely church in good heart.

Llanynys is, of course, in the diocese of St Asaph just a few miles up the road. The cathedral is best known for being the smallest in England and Wales but other claims to fame include its burning by Owain Glyndŵr in 1402, the possession of a William Morgan Welsh Bible in its museum, along with a Welsh-Hebrew-Greek Dictionary written by Dic Aberdaron, the Gwynedd tramp who spoke thirty-five different languages, and a monument to the memory of Mrs Hemans, the poetess who wrote new versions of ancient Welsh legends. Last, but by no means least, it is the home of the St Asaph Music Festival, which, under the able and inspired direction of composer Professor William Mathias, delights audiences from as far afield as Liverpool, Manchester, mid-Wales and Anglesey for a week every September. On our last visit the Halle Orchestra were playing Wagner, Brahms and Beethoven. Is it any wonder we chose Glyndŵr Country for our holidays?

Castle Street, Ruthin.   Photo: F. Leonard Jackson

RUTHIN

Ruthin was the town Owain Glyndŵr chose as his first target. It was a 20-mile march over hills and moorland and the Children of Owain, as his army came to be known, must have made a brave sight as they strode behind his banner. Some had bows and arrows, some swords and others the traditional North Wales weapon, the spear. Those who couldn't afford arms carried sickles.

The day they chose was 18 September, 1400, two days after Owain assumed the title of Prince of Wales and three days before the town's great annual event, the St Matthew's Day Fair. Owain's army arrived after dark and waited for dawn in Coedmarchan Forest at the back of the castle.

When the town gate was opened the Children rushed in to pillage and burn. They chose their time well. Booths had been set up in readiness for the biggest cloth and shoe market in its day in north-east Wales. No-one was killed in the raid but the town was put to the torch. The subsequent coroner's jury estimated the damage at £12,000, a fortune in medieval times. The only buildings in the town to survive the raid were No. 2 Well St and the Castle.

There was no mention at the inquest of Lord Reginald de Grey, the castle's owner, so it must be assumed he was away when his town was sacked. But the speed with which the fourteen rebels who were caught were executed suggests his swift intervention.

Even in his absense the Children of Owain could not get access to the great red castle. It is a ruin now but enough remains — including the dungeons where Owain's supporters were hanged — to show how powerful it was. In de Grey's day it had two wards separated by a dry fosse, cut in the sandstone, which can still be seen, and linked by a wooden suspension bridge. The larger outer ward was five-sided, its Gate of Entrance flanked by two massive towers. Under these were the dungeons and next to them the castle well. Behind the north wall was de Grey's baronial hall and court of justice. Five more towers were connected by a boulevard.

Grey's Marcher castle, built by an ancestor between 1277 and 1284 in the reign of Edward I, was not the first defensive building on the site. Before ever stone was laid the land was known as "Erw trwm lwyth", the acre with the heavy load on it, an allusion, no doubt, to the presence of a Welsh fort.

In 1508 George de Grey, the fifth baron, crippled by gambling debts, sold the castle and lordship of Ruthin to the crown. In the following century it was bought, like so many other properties in this part of the world, by the Myddeltons. It survived the Civil Wars — and a three-month siege — but, along with other fortresses, became the victim of a Cromwellian demolition order and was finally pulled down in 1648.

In 1826, through marriage, the estate was allied with the West family, later the Cornwallis-Wests. The Myddelton-West line was eventually to peter out in disgrace with the suicide, in 1951, of the son of the house, George Cornwallis-West, but at least during these years the castle had been rebuilt, proud and handsome, in local red sandstone.

George's mother was the infamous Patsy Cornwallis-West and even now in Ruthin the few people who can remember her still call her "The Bitch". She was spoilt and autocratic. She refused to allow cooking in the castle. Food was cooked in a kitchen near the Wynnstay Arms and taken to the castle. She was the daughter of a Dublin clergyman. When she married the ultra-respectable Colonel William Cornwallis-West she was 16. Her husband was 41. By the time she was 21 she had given birth to three children. They were known as the Wild West Show. One of them, the hapless George, was almost certainly the son of his mother's lover the Prince of Wales, later to become Edward VII, who stood as his godfather. One daughter became Princess of Pless, the other the first of the four wives of "Bend Or", the fabulously wealthy second Duke of Westminster.

But it was George who made the most startling match of all. His mother's rival was Winston Churchill's mother, the promiscuous Lady Randolph Churchill, whose 200 indentified lovers also included Edward VII. In 1899 Edward brought Lady Randy, as she was known, to visit Patsy Cornwallis-West at Ruthin. To everyone's amazement son George fell for and subsequently married her. In 1913 they were divorced and two hours after the divorce became absolute George married a leading actress, Mrs Patrick Campbell. The bride, on whom George Bernard Shaw doted, was not best pleased to discover she had married a bankrupt ne'er do well who had run through a fortune of £132,750 and borrowed £8,000 from fellow officers in the Guards. When he shot himself in 1951 he was described as a rogue, an amorous fool and victim of the set into which he was born. He still had some distance to go to be as appalling as his mother, though he did his best. He walked out on Mrs Campbell owing her £9,000, leaving her to die in penury and marrying a wealthy widow on the day of her memorial service.

His mother was known, with some justice, as the wickedest woman in Wales. Spiteful and selfish, she revelled in her nymphomania. When she was sixty-three her voracious appetites almost brought down Lloyd George's government. She was visiting wounded soldiers at Denbigh Hospital, no doubt looking for prey, when she was attracted by a handsome young private called Barrett. Through friends in high office at the War Ministry she had him moved to Ruthin Castle and promoted from the ranks to second lieutenant. Barrett, who was 27, was scandalised at the idea of making love to an elderly lady and made it quite clear he wasn't interested. It came near to costing him his life. Enraged, Patsy turned once again to her friends in the War Office screaming for blood. Some very senior officers obliged and the luckless Barrett found himself being posted to the most dangerous sector of the Western Front. But the scandal broke in the press, the government trembled and Lloyd George acted swiftly. A number of senior officers left the army hurriedly. Lieutenant Barrett was recalled and Mrs Cornwallis-West faded into a richly deserved obscurity.

She and her unfortunate husband, while they had little taste in human beings, were much better in design. They created an exquisite setting for their outrageous life, transforming the castle into the elegant building in which we stayed on our tour of Glyndŵr Country. Happily Ruthin Castle is in much more respectable hands today, in fact in the hands of old friends of ours, the Warburton family. Ian was with Terry, the head of the family, at the auction sale where, on a whim, he bought the castle — he had actually gone to buy the manorial title as a present for his wife.

Since then he has turned what was a white elephant into a hotel with an international reputation and he has opened a conference suite that regularly caters for 120 delegates at a time from all over the world.

The Castle stands in 30 acres of parkland with the unusual attractions of dungeons, a drowning pool and a whipping pit; a flock of peacocks and their less gaudy mates, a dovecote and an aviary.

Neither of us can remember ever having been in a more elegant cocktail bar than the panelled octagonal room at Ruthin which, in the Cornwallis-West's day, was the castle library. Traditionally libraries in Victorian days were places of assignation. Our assignation there was with other guests assembling for the medieval banquet which Terry introduced as a temporary attraction a quarter of a century ago and has been held virtually every night of the year since.

The night we went, there were guests in the banqueting hall from the U.S.A., Canada, Taiwan, the Phillipines, Iran, India, Russia and Australia. Every night a couple are chosen as Baron and Consort. They sit in thrones on a raised dais as Lord and Lady of the Feast. The night we were there the honour went to a French Canadian businessman, Robert Lapierre and his wife Jeannine.

Medieval banquets are tricky things to present. They so easily become arch and embarrassing. Ruthin does not. It might be the decor which is almost theatrically medieval; it might be the menu which has four removes (on the night we were there, vegetable soup, roast lamb, half a chicken roasted in honey and a compote of fruit and wine). We are inclined to think it is the staff who give the banquet its atmosphere. They are all local people and, like most Welshmen and women, actors manques. The waitresses sang between courses, the Herald was as to the manor born. A local man, Hugh Jones, played the musical saw and sent on to give a brilliant parody of Sosban Fach, a Welsh nonsense song, in three different versions — North Walian, South Walian and Russian.

Ian won a prize for writing rude limericks. But the best thing about the evening, he insists, was eating with his fingers as everyone did in the Middle Ages. He discovered the joys of tactile eating and maintains there is something deeply satisfying in ripping apart a roast chicken. Celia was afraid, as the evening went on, he was regressing to some Dark Age Welsh ancestor.

It is a very strange sensation to wander round the immaculately kept gardens and the gently undulating park of Ruthin Castle, step through the gates and find yourself in the bustle and rush of this enchanting little town. It is particularly delightful on Wednesdays in summer. Ken Favell, a local architect who created the banquets, also organised a Medieval Fair where local people wear medieval and Tudor costumes, old trades are piled and there is a market which must look not unlike the one Glyndŵr raided. There is a genuine survivor of those times in another market to which the town still owes much of its prosperity and which flourishes every Thursday and Friday.

The glory of Ruthin is the street of fine houses that leads from the castle to the market place. The finest of the buildings is Nantclwyd House, which was the home of Gabriel Goodman who was born there in 1528. His friends included some of the finest minds of the Elizabethan age. Through one of them William Cecil, the Queen's first minister, he became Dean of Westminster and a zealous burner of Puritans.

His house is a fine example of the Tudor period but there are traces from a much earlier period of rock and wattle and daub. In the hall there is a fine oak fireplace, panelling and a magnificent gallery. Until recently the house provided judges from the Assizes with superlative lodgings and there are now plans by its owners, Clwyd County Council, to turn it into a museum. We just hope when they do they demand the return of the wooden panel portraits of the Goodman family which were unaccountably left to the National Museum in Cardiff where they remain unseen in the cellars.

Ian has fond memories of the friendly Assizes in the town when the Head Boy of Ruthin School traditionally presented a Latin Address to the judge requesting a half holiday for his school and was then invited to the sumptuous Judge's Breakfast at Nantclwyd House.

The Old Courthouse on the square, which is now the National Westminster Bank, is another fine early building. It can be recognised by the gibbet projecting from its north-west wall. Business was literally executed on the spot. Prisoners were kept in cells below the magnificent court room with its impressive great beams.

In 1775 a new courthouse was built and in the nineteenth century it was rebuilt. It is now the public library but in its time it was considered a model. In his admirable book on

Ruthin a local bookseller and historian Keith Kenyon-Thompson estimates that on the treadmill there the prisoners did the equivalent of climbing 12,000 feet every day. Special punishments were laid down for swearing and blaspheming.

St Peter's Church, behind another glorious example of ornamental iron gates by the Davies Brothers of Bersham, dates back to 1284 when it was founded as a collegiate church. The office of Warden, which still exists today, dates from that period.

The glory of the church is its fine black oak roof with 408 panels, each one carved with a different armorial device, some dating to the reign of Richard III. Popular tradition has it that the roof was brought here from Basingwerk Abbey on the orders of Henry VII who bought the castle from the gambling de Grey of the day. The double nave in the present church dates bach to 1310. There are only two church spires in the Vale of Clwyd. Fittingly one of them is on St Peter's Church.

Exmewe Hall, now Barclays Bank, survived, in part at least, the raid of Owain's Children and is an interesting building of the late medieval period. Outside is Maen Huail, a huge, roughly dressed stone. It commemorates one of King Arthur's less chivalrous moments.

Huail was the brother of Gildas, a great chieftain. He courted a lady of whom Arthur was enamoured. Arthur armed himself secretly and ambushed Huail on his way to the lady's house. They fought and Huail drew first blood by wounding Arthur in the thigh. The duel ended and Huail promised never to refer to the time he beat the king in combat. The blow gave Arthur a permanent limp. Some years late he fell for another lady in Ruthin and went to see her disguised as a woman. One day when the lady and her maids and the king in drag were dancing together Huail came upon them. He recognised the king and said with a sneer, "The dancing may pass muster but for the stiff thigh." Arthur heard him and was so upset at being discovered dressed as a woman that he had Huail beheaded on Maen Huail (Huail's Stone). On hearing of this Gildas, Huail's brother, who was in Ireland, returned to Wales and raised such a storm that Arthur was forced to hand over his estate in Denbighshire as a blood fine.

Another execution in Ruthin that was brought to the public's attention in 1987 was that of the martyr Charles Meehan, a Franciscan priest from Ireland who was among 85 British martyrs to be declared "Blessed" by Pope John Paul II at a special Vatican mass that year. The ceremony, where two other martyrs from Wales were beautified (the first step to sainthood), was historic too for the Welsh language. For the first time it was used in the Vatican. Meehan was among the most unfortunate of martyrs. He had been returning home to Ireland from Rome in 1673 when he was shipwrecked off the Denbighshire coast. He was arrested with incriminating books and papers in his possession — Catholicism was outlawed in Britian at the time — and was executed at Ruthin the following year.

At one time there were sixty inns and public houses in Ruthin, some with delightful names like "The Slip Inn and Slap Out", where older boys from Ruthin School used to slip in for a drink and he slapped out by a master. Others included "The Bunch of Violets", in a far from sweet-smelling stable yard, and "Yr Iwerddon", which means Ireland and refers to the Irish cattle dealers who stayed there. These have all disappeared but the Wynnstay Arms remains, where George Borrow bought John Jones, a weaver with whom he had walked from Llangollen, the first roast duck he had eaten in his life.

St Peter's Square, is the most elegant square in Glyndŵr Country. Even with the traffic it is still pleasant on a warm day in spring or autumn to sit outside one of the fine inns or stroll round the stalls of the market. In earlier times bulls were baited there in front of one of the nine pubs which used to flourish in the square — in Ruthin there was once a pub for every ten males in the population.

The Myddelton Arms was called the "Eyes of Ruthin" by virtue of the cluster of dormer windows. Although the frontage is Georgian the building dates from the mid-sixteenth century. It was built by Sir Richard Clough, an Elizabethan merchant who employed Dutch builders, which explains the unusual architecture.

Our favourite spot in Ruthin, though, was the churchyard with the fine headmaster's house and Christ's Hospital which are pure "Barchester Towers". The Old Grammar School buildings there reminded us that Ruthin School, is still alive and well, independent and teaching fifteen subjects to GCSE and eighteen to 'A' level. It has both day pupils and boarders and takes girls as well as boys, something which would have shocked its founders in the thirteenth century. It has impressive new buildings on the Mold Rd.

On our way out of Ruthin — where, incidentally, a curfew bell still tolls at 8 p.m. every evening, the last town in Britain where this happens — we stopped to browse and shop at the Ruthin Craft Centre, a charming garden-plaza surrounded by fourteen craft workshops and an art gallery. Earlier Celia had both browsed and bought in the elegant town centre shops. In the last few years Ruthin has made a name for itself in the fashion world and many women looking for smart and up-to-the-minute day and evening wear now prefer to shop in the town's several boutiques than journey to Chester.

At Eyarth Old Railway Station just outside Ruthin at Llanfair D.C. is the world's best bed and breakfast. It is owned and has been converted into a guest house by the Spencer family. It was awarded the title in 1988 by the "Worldwide Bed and Breakfast Association."

Our destination on leaving Ruthin was the country park at Moel Famau. Moel Famau (Mother Mountain) is the highest peak in the Clwydian Range, where there are twenty more ancient hill forts. On a clear day from its 1,820 ft summit there are panoramic views of the estuaries of the Dee and the Mersey, the North Wales coast, Cader Idris and the Wrekin. Also on its summit can be seen the remains of a tower built to commemorate fifty years of the reign of George III.

The best way to reach it is from the village of Llanbedr Dyffryn Clwyd, where, incidentally, at the shooting lodge, Plas y Nant, Edward VII used to entertain his girl-friends. If he had been around to-day, he would certainly have appreciated the superb high cuisine of Llanbedr Hall. The road from the village up the hillside gives spectacular views of the Clwydians. After picnicking in the Country Park at one of the many sites in the forest, Celia and the dog Kip walked down through the woods to Glyndŵr Country's other fine Country Park at Loggerheads. Ian drove the car further along the Mold road through Llanferres, which has a delightful church first built in the thirteenth century, to Llanarmon-yn-Iâl for an envious look at Tomen-y-Faedre, a moated house which is on the site of a Norman castle. Fittingly in the church there is a fine effigy of a crusader and a mural to a cavalier.

From there he drove on to find one of his favourite stretches of woodland in Wales, the Nant-y-Garth Pass, and on to Llandegla, a moorland village which was famous all over Wales for St Tegla's Well where pilgrims were cured of epilepsy by bathing in its waters, throwing in coins and reciting the Lord's Prayer.

The Llandegla Moors are studded with drovers' pubs and it was at one of these in Loggerheads that Ian and Celia met up again. The bar parlour of the pub was heavily populated by a brace of terrier pups when Ian arrived — two terriers equal forty couples of any other dog — to find Celia sitting under the original inn-sign showing two people at "loggerheads". It was painted by the father of English landscape painters, Richard Wilson, who, they remembered, had painted the waterfall "with sheeps" at Chirk Castle. He must have had a fine sense of humour.

The next stop was Mold and a visit to the admirable Theatr Clwyd, part of the County Council project which was the brain child of Haydn Rees, a remarkable Chief Executive of the Council who went on to run the Wales Water Board.

It is a fine theatre with a programme which varies from light plays with West End stars to very experimental theatre indeed. The complex is quite splendid and worth a visit just to prove that not all modern architecture is banal. The Assize Courts are pure theatre too, with what we can only describe as a triumphal staircase leading up to the immense glass frontage. Higher on the hill is the theatre itself, a television studio with better facilities than many networks and one which is in constant professional use, and a network of art galleries.

But in view of our final destination on our tour of Glyndŵr Country we thought it wise the next day after a delicious pub lunch at Loggerheads Inn to return to the Country Park across the road. We were glad we did, and not only for the enchanting walk along the banks of the Alun, winding slowly through picturesque and varied woodland along the steep cliffside.

In the summer there are many places in Wales to enjoy. But in spring and autumn Glyndŵr Country is beyond compare. We went to Loggerheads on a bright October day — September and October are usually fine in North Wales — and we were stunned by the beauty around us. Loggerheads is a good place to enjoy either spring or autumn. The air tastes like a good Chablis, the waters sparkle in the fresh, clear light those seasons enjoy and the autumn leaves, fragile and transparent, shine like golden rice paper. More practically, the walks through the trees are admirably laid and we saw wheelchairs being pushed along them with ease. School parties examined with minute attention flora and fauna and all was well in this little world.

Happily the Council Department which planned and created this delightful park has a fine sense of style. When we visited in 1987 the Interpretive Centre and restaurant were still being built but it was a delight to remark how sympathetically they melted into their surroundings. We cannot wait to go back when the cafe is open and the exhibitions on show.

Our last night in Glyndŵr Country was an act of total self-indulgence. We spent it at an Italian Palace in the heart of the Welsh countryside on the outskirts of Mold.

Soughton Hall was built in the early eighteenth century by Edward Conwy of Bodrhyddan, near Rhyl. In 1732 he sold the estate to a kinsman who was Bishop of St Asaph. Its owners have included two knights, a bishop, a chaplain to Queen Victoria, an Appeal Court judge and three high sheriffs of Flintshire. Embellishments made later to the Hall reflect the influence the Grand Tour of Europe had on the gentlemen of the day, for Soughton is a mirror image of an Italian palazzo.

In 1986 Rosemary and John Rodenhurst, their son Simon, a champion runner, and schoolgirl daughter Penny moved in. John had been farming in Shropshire but they decided what they really wanted to do was create the sort of hotel they would most like to stay in. Soughton Hall was on the market so they sold their two farms and bought it. For the Rodenhursts it was the end of a 400-year-old tradition but John felt the traditional farmer's way of life was disappearing anyway.

When they moved in the house was slipping rapidly into dereliction. John hired local brickies, plumbers, joiners and electricians, who stopped the dry rot, mended the holes in the roof, laid a mile of central heating pipes and another mile of electric cable. Rosemary travelled thirty thousand miles looking for antique furniture and luxurious modern fabrics and, incredibly, with the family working sixteen hours a day, in less than a year the restoration was complete. The result is not so much living in an hotel as going to stay with very rich friends. There is a tiny cocktail bar where once the squire's court was held but most of the guests drink in the comfortable, country house drawing room which adjoins it. In the grand Drawing Room upstairs, under a painted beam ceiling, bearing a massive, crystal chandelier, the walls are hung with copies of the medieval Virgin and the Unicorn tapestries, which we last saw in Paris in the Musée de Cluny. The Rubens Room, which is now the restaurant, seats only fifty guests and has a Regency painted trompe d'oeil ceiling. High windows are sheltered by luxurious drapes, the walls are clad in French-designed fabric and the glassware on the tables is rock crystal. Once there was a Rubens cartoon on the wall.

The chef, Malcolm Warham, trained at Gleneagles Hotel and worked in Paris. Every one of the ten bedroom suites is furnished with antiques. A table bears bottles of Decantae spring water from the Clwyd hills and a bowl of fruit. In the wardrobe are scented coat hangers, bowls of pot-pourri stand on the mantlepiece, along with pretty vases, trinket boxes and — most useful — a mending kit. Each room has a trouser press and the bathrooms, with flowered basins, gold tap fittings, sweet-smelling soaps and shower gels and soft, thick bathrobes are a sheer delight.

We looked from our windows across the reclaimed gardens and the park and it did seem that if a tour of Glyndŵr Country has got to end, it could not happen in a better place. Our tour from Bala to Mold had been the happiest holiday of a lifetime.